T0167960

Praise for *Why You Dread Work*

An engaging and well-researched look at why too many people dread their jobs and what to do about it. Packed with wisdom, this book offers practical advice for making work better.
Professor Amy Edmondson, Harvard Business School; author
of *The Fearless Organization: Creating Psychological Safety
in the Workplace for Learning, Innovation, and Growth*

What a novel and entertaining book this is! It is very well written and answers the question so many people ask about 'why you dread work', and more importantly, what you can do about it. It is a 'must read' for those looking to get greater satisfaction from work and for employers interested in workplace wellbeing.
Professor Sir Cary Cooper, 50th Anniversary
Professor of Organizational Psychology & Health,
ALLIANCE Manchester Business School

A vital guide to help you and your colleagues work better.
Rory Sutherland, vice chairman of Ogilvy UK and author of
Alchemy: The Surprising Power of Ideas That Don't Make Sense

Why You Dread Work is a thoroughly enjoyable read. Containing great research to back up its key points, it provides chilling insights into the damage organizations can do. It will make workers realize they are not alone and is a must read for managers if they want to avoid the pitfalls Holmes identifies!
Dr Kay Maddox-Daines, Head of School for
People Management at Arden University

Why You Dread Work

PERSPECTIVES ON BUSINESS

Series editor: Professor Diane Coyle

Why You Dread Work: What's Going Wrong in Your Workplace and How to Fix It — Helen Holmes

Digital Transformation at Scale: Why the Strategy Is Delivery (Second Edition) — Andrew Greenway, Ben Terrett, Mike Bracken and Tom Loosemore

Why You Dread Work

What's Going Wrong in Your Workplace and How to Fix It

Helen Holmes

LONDON PUBLISHING PARTNERSHIP

Copyright © 2021 Helen Holmes Ltd

Published by London Publishing Partnership
www.londonpublishingpartnership.co.uk

Published in association with
Enlightenment Economics
www.enlightenmenteconomics.com

All Rights Reserved

ISBN: 978-1-913019-22-8 (pbk)
ISBN: 978-1-913019-23-5 (iPDF)
ISBN: 978-1-913019-24-2 (epub)

A catalogue record for this book is
available from the British Library

This book has been composed in Candara

Copy-edited and typeset by
T&T Productions Ltd, London
www.tandtproductions.com

Printed and bound by TJ Books Ltd, Padstow

Contents

Author's note

A lot of people generously contributed their workplace experiences to this book; where necessary these have been anonymized. Some details have also been changed: for example, the trust workshop that I describe is a composite of various workshops to help preserve the anonymity of those who participated (who, where featured, did also give me permission to describe their stories). The words of interviewees are otherwise as spoken or written.

Why You Dread Work

Introduction

M any of us have experienced Sunday night dread: the lurking disquiet that another working week is just around the corner.

But what is driving it? Ironically, the dread is rarely to do with your actual role. Being hired to do something and then being allowed to get on with it is a relatively simple business. Where work seems to get tricky is with *everything else* – other people, politics, tricky interactions, competing priorities and constant change.

Or maybe it's just you? Everyone else seems OK.

It's not just you.

In one 2019 survey, no less than 81% of employees said they experienced Sunday night dread. So, how can I put this? Despite the sincere efforts of HR departments and executive boards all over the world, many workplaces still generate a startling amount of stress and discontent, whether it's due to a defensive colleague, an anxious boss or that crazy decision the sales director just made. (Of course, your workplace may not even be a physical environment – you may work from home, yet find to your chagrin that working remotely doesn't confer any immunity from dreading Monday morning.)

Your company knows full well that workplace culture matters: it has mission statements and lists of values coming out of its ears. It runs 'well-being webinars' designed to keep you happy and productive. It champions the rational ideal of teamwork, collaboration and engaged, driven colleagues. So why does your working week remain so frustrating, anxiety-inducing or even downright bizarre? What's going on?

We also don't reflect enough on how *strange* workplaces can be. This is partly because the culture and climate of an organization can feel somewhat elusive and subjective, especially when you're right in the middle of them.* Maybe it's just the way things are: the price of employment. Or perhaps we're simply too busy and tired to think about anything more than what we're going to have for dinner.

But does working life really have to be this way?

In this book, I explore what brings on that horrible Sunday night dread. What can make even a well-intentioned organization a dispiriting place, and why does it happen? More importantly, how can workplaces become better, happier environments in which to invest our time?

I'm interested in how we can all build a better working week because I have a double life (not the thrilling, superhero kind). As well as being an author and satirical journalist, I also have twenty years' experience in technology organizations, from my first job for a small software company (where, for a while, I had the dubious honour of being the lowest-paid person in the whole company – trust me, I saw the payroll spreadsheet) to VP/director level in international financial technology firms. My background is in product management: a role that involves interaction with nearly every department in a business.

However, any experience of my own immediately pales into insignificance when I tell other people I'm writing a book about the trials of the modern workplace. Even my calmest, most sanguine of friends – including those who work in academia or for charities – launch into spirited anecdotes that include

---

* They even feel elusive and subjective to experts, with 31,500 results on Google debating the difference between workplace culture and workplace climate alone. It is helpful to think of company culture as an organization's personality ('how things get done around here'), while climate is more localized and ephemeral (e.g. the mood of a specific team).

phrases such as, 'And you won't *believe* what he said next!' It soon becomes clear that every company – from the smallest non-profit to the biggest investment bank – regularly makes its employees want to bang their heads against their screens and retreat to live in a small hut, deep in a forest somewhere.

While dutifully writing things down and contemplating retraining as a therapist, it becomes clear to me that improving the working week is a huge topic. It's impossible to explore every angle, but happily, what I'm interested in is very simple: What impacts people the most? What do they rant about to their partner or their flatmates every evening?

It's often not the obvious or logical parts of working life that cause all the trouble. Consultants Gerard Egan and William Tate have both written of companies as having a 'shadow side', described marvellously by Tate as 'the often disagreeable, messy, crazy and opaque aspects of your organisation's personality'. He adds that its features are 'always slippery – easier to feel than to define'. This book attempts to pin down the sources of workplace dread by grouping them into three sections.

- *Fear*: the problems that stem from insecurity, and their subtle ripple effects.
- *Focus*: how hard it is to get things done in a world of overdrive and constant change.
- *Fairness*: or, more accurately, how it feels when your organization is *not* being fair.

While I like the fact that these all begin with the letter 'f', thus making me appear to be some kind of hotshot consultant, these issues really are the ones that crop up most often in discussions of workplace unhappiness. This book doesn't highlight every possible workplace problem, of course. It focuses on the white-collar, knowledge-worker environment, and as such it views the world through an admittedly specific, narrow lens. However, where possible, the issues covered apply regardless of size or sector.

WHY YOU DREAD WORK

I also want to acknowledge the inconvenient obstacles that sit in the way of a lovely, utopian workplace. Is it realistic for the human needs of employees to coexist with the pursuit of profit? Can we really build the workplaces that we want? After all, not every company is willing to transform itself. Some are too unwieldy or too entrenched in their ways. For this reason this book does not focus on radical changes to organizational design, such as abolishing the workplace hierarchy in favour of self-managing teams. While this is fascinating territory, there are wonderful books on this already (e.g. Frederic Laloux's *Reinventing Organizations*).

Neither does this book focus solely on the kind of action that must be taken by an executive board. There are lots of great books out there that tell the inspirational tale of start-up X or give instructions on building the perfect team. But the executive board is not the only group that can change things – individuals can, too. So this book is written for the employees somewhere *in the middle of* an organization; for those who are too busy to step back and wonder if it's just them or whether their workplace feels a bit crazy. My aim is to offer tea and sympathy (virtually speaking), as well as some actionable suggestions for change.

What will you learn in this book? Well, a number of questions tend to come into your mind around 10 p.m. on a Sunday (one being 'Should I quit and open a llama trekking retreat in deepest Wales?'). I seek to answer the following.

- My company feels hard going. Is it just me?
- What's going wrong and why?
- Can things get better? What if my organization doesn't want to change?

The book draws deeply on people's experiences of their workplaces, and also shares some of the fascinating research done by academics and researchers all over the world into how workplaces function – or do not. Finally, I highlight the stories of some of the companies and individuals who are working to make Monday mornings a positive experience.

At the end of each part of the book there are two sets of ideas and tips. Firstly, there are some for your organization. Assuming you are not in charge yourself, these are the bits you can circle in highlighter pen and leave pointedly on your manager's desk, or upon that of your favourite HR person.

However, if you suspect you're a lone warrior in the quest for a better working week, there are also ideas that apply to you and your immediate team. While companies can initiate top-down transformation, you can also drive small improvements yourself. You can be a cultural rebel, building a little oasis of sanity amongst the chaos. (If challenged, please feel free to blame me and the bad influence of this book.)

What I really want is for anyone experiencing challenges at work to feel less alone. No matter where they work, or how high up the organizational ladder they are, everyone seems to experience similar frustrations, and that's got to be comforting in itself.

So where to start? Well, Sunday night dread could be interpreted as a mild inconvenience – awkward but tolerable, simply a sense that 'free time' is soon to turn into 'work time'. That is, until you isolate the word 'dread'. Dread is a gut-wrenching, physical thing – so let's start with a key cause: fear and insecurity.

PART I

FEAR

Chapter 1

Other people

After being in business for a number of years, many organizations are graced with the dubious honour of some kind of scandal: a punch-up, a torrid and highly visible liaison, a stapler chucked across the office in a wild rage.

I'm not talking about those stories.*

I'm interested in *low-level* bad behaviour: those apparently minor frustrations that appear to be routine, possibly even sanctioned by a business. Take simple, old-fashioned lack of civility.

Rudeness

One evening I go to see the comedian Michelle Wolf at the Leicester Square Theatre in London. She's vivacious, sharp and holds the crowd captivated. As I always make the mistake of thinking other people spring fully formed to greatness, I'm surprised to learn that Michelle had a very different life before stand-up comedy: she used to work on Wall Street, first for Bear Stearns and then, after its acquisition, for JP Morgan.

Michelle has said of her experience there: 'The way that my job on Wall Street helped me [with stand-up] is that, in the corporate world in general, sometimes people are so mean to you for absolutely no reason, and you just can't take it personally.

---

* Regrettably, most of the anecdotes I hear are unprintable, unbelievable or both.

People used to yell at me all the time, right in my face, and you just learn that it's not about you. That helps in comedy a lot.'

I suppose it's helpful that corporate life gave Michelle the resilience required for the gruelling business of stand-up, but – seriously? Why did she have to learn this from colleagues – adults in a highly professional environment? What happened to common civility?

Workplace rudeness is on the rise: 96% of US employees have been subject to workplace incivility and 99% have witnessed it. Between 1998 and 2005 the number saying they were treated rudely once or more per week almost doubled.

A head of marketing at a consultancy tells me, 'My boss openly criticises people in the business, all the time. He regularly calls people stupid or demeans the junior members of my team when they present to him. He snaps things like, "if you're just going to read out the slide, don't bother".'

Another executive took voluntary redundancy from a professional services firm after 'battling' a new boss, based in the US, who never met her face to face: 'My first ever encounter with him was when he phoned me up and was yelling down the phone. I still don't know what I had done wrong.'

It's crushing when you come to realize that rude people and bullies don't disappear when you leave the playground behind: you just about recover from the first bunch at school only to encounter them again in the workplace. In fact, the workplace is a bit like school: it's the same, arbitrary throwing-together of very different personalities. You all have to get along, but how will it pan out? Those hopeful that reason and justice will prevail are probably the same ones who used to get their lunch money stolen.

On occasion, you may suspect that people missed out on their true vocation of a career in the dramatic arts. A VP of Programme Management tells me, 'I had a boss who would say things like, "we're going to take a baseball bat to so-and-so", or yell that we'd all go to prison if something didn't get done. That was his actual terminology.'

Of course, not everyone is horrible: most people in a workplace are lovely. However, it only takes a few rotten apples to ruin someone's day. And an abrasive attitude spreads. Christine Pearson and Christine Porath, the authors of *The Cost of Bad Behavior*, are experts in how workers react when treated rudely. In one study, they found that 25% of managers who admitted to having behaved badly said they had been uncivil because their own leaders acted rudely.

Perhaps there is a leader further up the ranks who is unpredictably fierce, which keeps everyone on edge. Perhaps he is jovial for a moment of small talk before launching into a sudden verbal tirade, meaning that everyone is constantly nervous in meetings. 'Sports-related chat … last night's restaurant … ha ha!' Then – SLAM! 'Why haven't you made your numbers?' This kind of leader prides themselves on being terrifying except with a few inner-circle chums. That's tough on everyone else, who soon finds there's no way to get through to them. That is, unless they invent a time machine, go back twenty years and somehow happen to be their best friend in college.

This stuff gives most sensible people a headache: it doesn't take any more time to be polite than it does to be abrasive, and bullying appears utterly superfluous to the business of making money. This means that most forms of rudeness are, quite simply, an unacceptable power play. Rudeness says: I am more important than you. I need this from you and I do not care about you – not even enough to be civil. Ouch!

Who hijacked my radical candour?

Why are these individuals tolerated? Sometimes, people are misusing the idea of constructive conflict, which has become a buzzword in management circles. It's one of those trendy, counterintuitive things, like it being fine to fail as long as you fail fast. Robust dialogue, candour, radical honesty – call it what you will – the idea is that companies discard their fake harmony in favour of constructive challenge, to get things out in the open. Olann Kerrison, a VP for a financial firm, loves the concept. 'I hate that culture of everyone nodding but no one actually agreeing,' he tells me. 'It makes a mockery of meetings. People are constantly kowtowing to each other, out of some misplaced desire to avoid conflict. Then, all the real decisions happen in the corridor afterwards, and others feel out of the loop.'

The problem with constructive conflict is not the rationale, which is unarguably sound, but the fact that it can get hijacked by abrasive people, or those with a political agenda of their own. The idea is that you critique ideas not people, but it appears that not everyone has got the memo.

One executive at an international media company tells me, 'I've seen some horrific deliveries of "feedback". In one example, the victim put the phone down, left his house for two hours to calm down and then booked a week off, because he couldn't bear to be at work. People have no idea of the damage they can do.'

A marketing director agrees, telling me of the time she saw a colleague openly criticized in a meeting: 'He struggled to work with me afterwards, because I'd seen him humiliated. The problem is that the damage doesn't stay contained in that moment – there's an invisible ripple effect. People carry it with them.'

One executive in an accountancy firm felt that ripple effect for himself: 'Once, in a meeting, I challenged a difficult peer about something he'd done wrong, keeping it neutral like you're supposed to. He lashed out with a personal attack. "You did this and that? I'm very disappointed in you." He made it utterly personal and emotive – all to distract from the fact he had made a mistake.'

When misused, robust dialogue gives people carte blanche to launch into unguarded criticism, protected by their assertion they're 'just telling it like it is'. Too often, someone is left blindsided by the very public criticism they've just received. This can also be a great way to wound people twice: first be rude to them and then, if they react, imply they're not strong enough to take honest feedback.

Before too long, you can almost forgive people for finding they miss their nice, fake harmony. After all, if your peers can verbally lash out at any moment, how safe is it to raise your hand or voice an idea?

Favourites

Abrasive behaviour sometimes goes unchecked because the perpetrator is a favourite of the boss, meaning they're pro-tected – even if they're unpleasant or inept.

A scientist working in the pharmaceutical industry tells me an all-too-familiar tale over lunch one day: 'It's a nightmare. My colleague is a favourite of my boss. If we criticize her, it lands on deaf ears.' Meanwhile, a senior manager in a travel firm tells me, 'This really rude guy is protected because he was brought in by the boss's boss. If he wasn't a favourite, he would be long gone.'

Favourites unbalance the team dynamic: if a leader listens to one individual at the expense of others, it weakens the unit. Their existence tells everyone that the company is an uneven playing field, with a selective communications channel. This kind of thing always makes me think of Henry VIII's penchant for propelling his current wife's ladies-in-waiting up to the (admit-tedly dubious) honour of being his next queen. He didn't have to respect anyone else's view, because he was in charge, but I bet there was some bitching around the court watercooler.*

Meanwhile, people see the most divisive individuals receiving extra perks, or sitting at the right hand of the CEO in meetings. As one sales director tells me glumly, 'It is depressing watching bad people thrive.'

---

* Not to mention at the Vatican.

Very occasionally, colleagues have a particular combination of traits that carries them into territory best described as 'damaged and damaging'. One 2010 study estimated that 3.9% of corporate professionals have psychopathic tendencies, compared with less than 1% of the general population. Management scholar Manfred Kets de Vries calls these individuals the 'Seductive Operational Bully', or 'psychopath lite'. He states, somewhat drily, 'they don't usually end up in jail or psychiatric hospital, but they do thrive in an organizational setting'.

These individuals' charm and ability to tell people what they want to hear serve them well in a corporate setting, and even negative traits can play in their favour. Kets de Vries states: 'A lack of remorse, guilt, and empathy can be used to advantage by Seductive Operational Bullies. They shine in situations that call for "tough" and unpopular decisions, such as [whether] to lay off staff.' Rather than being judged as dangerous, these employees may simply be considered 'difficult-to-manage high potentials' – leaving their colleagues dreading being around them.

Shockingly, it is even rumoured that some finance firms purposefully recruit social psychopaths because they are ideally suited to senior roles. 'At interview, they do psychometric testing and really look at what drives you,' one industry veteran tells me, 'But they're not looking for balance – they're looking for damage.'

'That's just what Jeff is like'

Why is it that people so often choose not to speak up about bullying or rudeness? Firstly, we humans are very good at adjusting to the norms around us – something that can do us a disservice in the workplace.

Secondly, people may assume they are the only one who finds the climate miserable, when actually their colleagues quietly feel the same way. When academics Christine Pearson and Christine Porath collected data from over 9,000 individuals across the

United States, they found that most employees concealed their feelings due to 'fear from possible repercussions and sounding soft'. Many felt nothing would be done, especially as 60% of the time, bad behaviour stemmed from higher up the ranks.

However, at some point, those further up the chain learn of a colleague's abrasiveness, perhaps via a complaint or a pattern of stress-related absence in the team. That's when an HR department needs to jump in, but sometimes there is no change at all. You may hear, 'Oh, that's just what Jeff is like.' (Note: difficult people are not always called Jeff. That would make it too easy.)

If a perpetrator gets good results, HR teams sometimes lack the support of the executive board to insist on behavioural change. One manager even tells me of a US-based individual who was fired by HR for bullying behaviour only to be summarily reinstated the next day by the company chairman, who was a sponsor. He says, 'The HR team still get complaints about her, but who are we trying to kid? It's pretty clear that they can't do anything.'

Board advisor and consultant Sue Kay has studied bad behaviour at board level across FTSE 250 businesses and is fascinated by the 'wilful blindness' that can occur. 'Businesses are often prepared to turn a blind eye to poor behaviour if those individuals are delivering results,' she tells me. Participants in her study felt that HR was 'not valued or listened to' or that they 'colluded with the line'. Kay observed that difficult people *would* be removed from the organization, but only if they failed in their business objectives.

In his 2013 report commissioned by Barclays Bank after their involvement in the Libor exchange rate scandal, veteran lawyer Anthony Salz found something similar. He stated: 'Heads of HR were typically on neither the Group nor divisional Executive Committees. HR appears accordingly to have found it difficult to exercise an appropriate level of challenge to the businesses on some people-related issues.'

Inaction at board level causes misery for the people caught in the orbit of a difficult colleague – and it can lead to bigger, reputational issues too. Susan Fowler, formerly an engineer at Uber, described in a 2017 blog post how senior management had ignored overt sexual harassment by her boss. Fowler's superiors told her he was a 'high performer' and they did not wish to punish what was 'probably just an innocent mistake'. Fowler later learned from other female engineers that this was not the individual's first offence. She wrote, 'We all gave up on Uber HR and our managers after that.' Fowler's blog post went viral, and the subsequent investigation and negative publicity were part of an avalanche of events that led to the resignation of Uber's CEO and significant reputational damage for the company.

There is, of course, an important distinction to make here. The abrasive are, generally, rogue agents, in that while they might get away with it, you won't find companies openly saying they embrace rudeness in their employees. You don't tend to find 'Be rude!' listed among a company's values. (Although perhaps the cheerful edict to 'Be yourself!' needs modifying to 'Be yourself – except if you're horrible'.)

Sometimes, however, tactics that drive a feeling of dread are validated by the structure of a workplace. Insecurity is not simply tolerated: it's baked in.

Competition

Imagine that this year you've got a one-in-ten chance of getting fired.

Once a year your company decides who falls within the lowest-performing 10% of employees, and those people are then asked to leave.

Feeling motivated?

Perhaps you are: perhaps it spurs you on to work harder. Personally speaking, this kind of thing makes me want to run screaming in the other direction, and that's probably why I don't work for one of the firms that still take the 'up or out' (or 'rank and yank') approach, popularized by General Electric boss Jack Welch in the 1980s. Every year, these companies (typically US legal, financial and consulting firms) cut the lowest-performing 5–10% of their workforces, in part to make way for new hires.

I'm told by an experienced wealth manager that, in his industry, it's a simple ratio between cost and earnings: 'In some years there can be even deeper cuts: in one year, four hundred people went from one bank. Another got rid of six hundred in a year.'

'Were those global figures?' I ask.

'No. That was just London.'

He recounts how, in practice, employees are invited to resign. 'There's a tap on the shoulder and you're told you're not making enough. You'll get severance pay and a good reference, but your time's up.'

Trading and sales roles are renowned for being high-stakes, high-reward. But even outside these firms, comparison or competition can be overtly deployed – perhaps by allowing an overlap in roles in order to spur fast results. One manager for a telecommunications company tells me: 'Someone on the executive board got the strategy team to produce "parallel" proposals for one project. It was a complete mess. Everyone was on the defensive, doing duplicate work, and hours were wasted on in-fighting instead of getting things done.'

There are also companies that explicitly rank their employees against their peers and then use these rankings to determine bonus allocation or other forms of reward. The advocates for this practice, known as stack ranking, are passionate, arguing that you can't reward the best performers without also identifying and acting upon poor performance.

If there are underperformers within an organization, then this certainly does need to be addressed. And of course companies want to identify high performers so they can reward strong contributions. However, as with so much in life, the concept struggles in implementation. The challenges creep in when a company has to determine what good or bad looks like. Employees are often still assessed on subjective assessments from their leader, or reduced to a plot point on a simplistic grid of objectives and behaviours. Sometimes a company requests that team members be placed on a defined curve: for example, 10% of the organization is to be ranked above average, 80% normal and 10% below par. However, where a team has many strong performers, this means that not all colleagues can be fairly rewarded. 'My lowest performer is at 120% of our team target for onboarding new clients,' one professional services team leader tells me. 'What am I supposed to do, mark them as a failure? Meanwhile, in another team, their top performer is only at 110%.'

Calibration exercises – where individuals' rankings are cross-referenced and adjusted across a broader peer group – are designed to help combat this disparity between teams, but new issues can creep in. Comparing individuals of the same grade but with different job titles means that the extra complexity of some roles goes unacknowledged. Calibration also raises a disquieting truth: if you only have a fixed bonus pot based on everyone achieving standard performance, then in order to reward a high performer, a low performer has to be found. Keen to secure more of the pot for their own team, the leaders of other teams may chip in with anecdotes that overemphasize single incidents or recent interactions. This is the dark side of the performance culture, and it leads to some unpleasant conversations in bonus allocation meetings:

> **Leader 1:** I rate my team member Matt as outstanding.
> **Leader 2:** Well, I emailed Matt one time and it took him three days to respond. I'd say he's below average. Whereas Sasha, in my team? She's excellent …

Those in favour of workplace competition argue that pressure provides impetus, helping innovation and speed to market.

Competition between teams can build cohesive units because colleagues have to become more interdependent. Pitting individuals against each other may fire people up with competitive spirit and allow managers to identify those most hungry for advancement.

Of course it is also possible that those at the top see competition as a de facto part of the workplace because that is how they scaled the ladder in the first place. In the United States in particular, with its strong cultural ideals of meritocracy and individualism, competition is ingrained from an early age. For example, grading techniques such as the bell curve award grades not on an absolute scale but relative to one's peers in class. By the time most Americans are adults, competition is the norm.

However, while highly effective in the marketplace, competition backfires in the workplace because it divides, and division weakens. The renowned Renaissance-era military tactician Niccolò Machiavelli was no stranger to ruthless tactics but even he presented 'divide and conquer' as a strategy for weakening enemies, not something to use on one's own foot soldiers. If colleagues are combatants, it's hard to be allies.

Indeed, instil too much rivalry and colleagues begin to see the workplace as a zero-sum game, where their own advancement can only come at the expense of someone else's. One marketing manager tells me: 'A colleague secretly got a rival agency to pitch for our website rebrand, then took the proposal to the marketing director to state that she should get my job instead. It didn't work – but I still have to work with her every day.'

Simon Worth, former CEO of the software company QAS Ltd, is scathing about internal competition: 'There's this theory that it helps you move faster, but it increases your risk of coming second. It distracts people from the idea of a shared goal and therefore detracts from your ability to create value.'

Apart from the practical fallout, there are people who simply hate competing. They experience competition not as a motivating force but as a threat: their safety compromised by the risk of failure; any sense of affinity or belonging crushed by being pitted against colleagues. Personally, I loathe having to jostle for resources with peers (and shudder when told of *Dragon's Den* style pitching battles for project funding, with a panel of board-level executives deciding who 'wins'). Even when I secure the resources I need, I always emerge from such contests feeling defeated: I want to be aiming at the same goal as my peers, not fighting them.

One potential dividing line is introversion and extroversion. One study by psychologist William Graziano showed that extroverts prefer those with whom they compete, while introverts favour those with whom they collaborate. Meanwhile, other research has linked competitive appetite to gender. In a study conducted by the Olin Business School, women performed as well as, or better than, male peers in non-competitive situations, but the introduction of competition reversed the results. Lead researcher Markus Baer said of the study: 'As soon as you introduce competition, forcing teams to compete with one another for resources or a prize, women perform worse. When you crank up the heat, women somehow stop doing the behaviors that help them succeed when they are working in a team.'

One theory, discussed by Ashley Merryman and Po Bronson in their book *Top Dog: The Science of Winning and Losing*, is that women rate their chances of success more realistically than men and compete only when they know they have a good chance of winning. Meanwhile, evolutionary biologists observe that women form close friendships and achieve this by finding common ground. Equality within the friendship is all-important (and it is maintained via lots of mirroring and self-deprecation). Why would a woman break this careful equilibrium by trying to come out on top?

Yet more studies propose that an appetite for competition, or the lack of one, may be shaped in the womb. One Italian study by Luigi Guiso and Aldo Rustichini correlated a predilection for entrepreneurship – with its attendant demands of risk-taking and readiness for competition – with the chemical wash of testosterone and oestrogen experienced in the womb by the developing brain of either male or female foetuses.

Regardless of where the aversion stems from, more and more businesses are acknowledging the downsides of the more overt forms of employee competition. Stack ranking is widely credited with creating an environment of rivalry. Companies like Microsoft and Amazon have dropped it, and the Institute of Corporate Productivity reports that just 14% of companies used it in the last decade, compared with 49% in the previous one. Officially, 'up or out' as a policy has also fallen out of favour, and it is no longer used by General Electric, who popularized it. Consultant Peter Cohan, writing in *Forbes*, states that it only worked when Jack Welch took over General Electric in the 1980s because 'the company had become fat and happy': there was fat to trim. In many of today's tightly run organizations, everyone is already talented. Binning the 'worst' is actually cutting into muscle: a waste of talent.

Hiring a large cohort of ambitious people and thinning them out is, however, still routine in several areas of corporate life, such as in US consultancies and law firms. And while stack ranking may not openly be described as such, companies still do it – they just keep iterating on the best way to compare employees.

Whatever it's called, a company that pits employees against each other shouldn't be surprised when collaboration suffers, because a sense of safety is important at a fundamental level. Take the work of Abraham Maslow, creator of the famous 'hierarchy of needs' way back in 1947.* Maslow theorized that a need

---

* Maslow's hierarchy of needs, introduced in 1947, laid out the different needs of an individual, starting with physiological needs and concluding with self-actualization, or the fulfilment of one's potential. He wrote it as a list but it is most commonly depicted as a pyramid, apparently since someone writing a business magazine article in the 1960s happened to draw it that way.

for safety was second only to basic physiological needs such as for food or oxygen. In safety he included the desire for order, control, freedom from fear, emotional security, financial security and a stable environment.

Right now, if someone came up to you in the street asking how they could gain a sense of control, freedom from fear and emotional security, would you point them in the direction of the nearest corporate workplace?

Chapter 2

The price of fear

One night, as a university student living in a ground-floor flat, I turned out my bedside lamp only to spot a middle-aged peeping Tom staring at me through a gap in my curtains. I still remember the jolt of shock as my eyes met his in the darkness. Had my response been rational, I would have run away, but for some reason I found myself leaping out of bed, running *towards* the window, flinging it open and yelling like a banshee. (The result: *he* ran away and I never saw him again.) I had heard of 'fight or flight' – a phrase coined by physiologist Walter B. Cannon in the 1920s to describe how people respond to fear at the instinctive, physiological level – but I had never before experienced it myself. Running towards the intruder happened in a split second, before I could consciously register what I was doing.

Years later I was to experience the contrary desire: to flee. This time I was at a big finance conference in Brussels, about to go onto the stage of a massive auditorium in front of several hundred people. New to the industry, I was one of about a dozen speakers scheduled to give a swift but particularly torturous kind of presentation called a *pecha kucha*, where your slides auto-rotate behind you as you speak, removing your control over the narrative. In retrospect, there had been warning signs. When I had signed up for the presentation, back in London, I'd had the following conversation at the coffee machine:

> **Sales manager:** Oh – Mike did that for us last year.
> **Me:** I don't think I've met Mike yet.
> **Sales manager** (faintly amused): Oh, he doesn't work for us
> any more. Not after that.

Apparently, Mike had walked off stage halfway through his presentation and left the business shortly afterwards.

Back in Brussels, the MC on stage was mischievously ramping up the tension (sample statement: 'Not only is your current boss in this audience, your next boss is too!'). When the presentations began, the man ahead of me lost his place halfway through his talk and, ashen-faced, repeated 'sorry – sorry' while his slides revolved uselessly behind him. Suddenly, my body decided it did not want to be there. I had to physically grip the underside of my seat so I couldn't pelt for the exit. I made it through my own talk but I was pretty atrocious, and the episode triggered a determination to become a better presenter.*

Both fighting and fleeing probably appear a little over the top for most workplace scenarios. Look around at your colleagues on an average day: whether you're in the office or on a video call, no one is going to announce that they're insecure. Everything seems normal enough. So what is the price of the humdrum, everyday kind of fear? How does it actually manifest at work? Well, you see it in a number of quiet, insidious ways. And none of them are good for business.

Fight: the snake pit

Fight? Not literally (apart from that notorious Christmas party back in 2007).

Colleagues are unlikely to pile in to a punch-up, but they do find different ways to fight back. For example, if placed in

---

* Later, I joined the advisory board of the conference organization. An early suggestion: scrap the scary presentation format.

competition, peers quickly become rivals rather than a source of vital mutual support.

An analyst in a consultancy where everyone was vying for promotion tells me: 'I once shared an anecdote with a colleague while chatting over breakfast before a workshop, only to have him bring up and then criticize what I had told him in the workshop itself. I learned pretty fast never to share anything with him again.' The analyst went on to tell me that he eventually found supportive peers, but it took time.

One sales manager in a property firm has a more blunt view. 'It's a snake pit,' he says frankly, 'I would sometimes like to ask my peers for advice but it's too risky. They all want our boss's job, and are desperate to show that they're the most likely candidate in his succession plan, so show any vulnerability at all and they'd be casually mentioning to the boss, "Oh, he asked for my help over coffee – I think he's struggling."'

Sometimes, of course, the price of fear is ... well, more fear. The philosopher Seneca wrote, 'All cruelty springs from weakness,' while a 2008 study on playground dynamics found that 90% of bullies were themselves being bullied. In the workplace, someone being awkward may be being pressured by someone more senior and it is cascading downwards. Or perhaps they've just been asked to do something without being granted sufficient time or budget. You just happen to be in their way.

The more high-stakes, high-reward an industry is, the more prevalent toxic behaviour becomes, as colleagues compete to secure coveted resources or rewards. One investment banker acknowledges that his industry is particularly cut-throat: 'You're never truly safe, not unless you work for yourself. You're always looking over your shoulder. Even now after ten years I'm afraid I'll get a tap on the shoulder. It does bring out the worst in people.'

Meanwhile, an executive in banking tells me that she can hear the stress in people's voices: 'When they shout, or no longer care how they talk to you, it's clear they are frightened and overwhelmed.'

One fascinating body of research into workplace dynamics centres on the 'masculinity contest culture', where respect is gained through dominating others. Workplaces like this overtly value qualities that Western cultures deem traditionally male. Sociologist Christin L. Munsch describes the masculinity contest as 'a set of organizational norms that fosters competition, work devotion, strength, and dominance'. They are associated with high stress, low engagement and an increased likelihood of job hunting. Crucially, while these organizational cultures are instigated by alpha males, they are not the only participants. In a culture defined by these values, everyone has to play by the same rules in order to thrive.

It may be significant that research in fields from psychology to sociology have described masculinity as a precarious characteristic. While being female is an ascribed characteristic – something the average woman doesn't really think much about – masculinity is seen in many cultures as an *earned* characteristic: something that must be proven, again and again. Psychologists Jennifer Bosson and Joseph Vandello describe the Western cultural perception of manhood as 'elusive and tenuous', writing, 'Put another way, "real men" are made, not born.' If manhood is conditional on the deference of others, then in a masculine workplace culture people *never feel entirely safe* in their position. Those working in this environment feel they must not only establish their dominance but also constantly maintain it.

Whatever its source, being on the receiving end of rudeness encourages people to fight back in a surprising variety of ways. In their work on incivility, Christine Pearson and Christine Porath found that employees are deeply impacted by rudeness, and quietly punish both the perpetrators and the companies that tolerate them. Their research shows that 48% of people who experience incivility purposefully reduce the effort they put into their work, 38% deliberately reduce their work quality, and 25% even report taking their frustration out on customers. In one study, merely being around uncivil colleagues made people more likely to have 'dysfunctional and aggressive' thoughts.

Some people take a more mischievous approach and indulge their urge to undermine or lightly sabotage their workmates. One individual tells me: 'A former Head of Legal was always really rude and dismissive around me. When she needed a new person in her team, I recommended someone from a former company whom I suspected would ultimately drive her up the wall. It worked. I felt so much better after that, especially after pocketing my employee referral bonus.'

Another tells me: 'I used to work with one guy who was obnoxious. In the end, I would wind him up on purpose. One time I sent him an email and just knew that within thirty seconds he would sweep, enraged, into my bit of the office. So I hid under the desk. He stomped in, looked confused, then had to leave again.'

To misquote the great Ferris Bueller, 'It's a little childish and stupid. But then, so is the workplace.'

Freeze: nothing to see here

It's actually 'fight, flight, freeze or fawn'. Did you know that? Psychologists have added to the original list, slightly ruining the nice, crisp symmetry of the first version. There are now *four* possible impulses when threatened. 'Freeze' immediately strikes me as apt in a workplace context because it describes how people can react when in a negative or unsafe environment. For example, it can translate into an inability to ask even the most basic questions.

Let's imagine that an abrupt and time-pressured CEO asks you for 'an update on commercial partnership X'. Everyone is thrown into chaos. What does he mean by 'an update'? Does he want an overview of all aspects of performance against the key performance indicators in the contract? Does he want a slide deck? How much detail does he want? The last thing that occurs to anyone is to simply ask him what he means, because *the CEO would think they were an idiot.*

This blind panic may not immediately seem like freezing: there's a lot of nervous movement going on. However, the key is not the panic, but the blindness. What you want is to move freely – ask questions, get more information, possibly even push back on the timeline – but the permitted framework is too rigid. You're paralysed by something as simple as an intimidating leader.

The result is that the twenty-minute update takes a team of people a fortnight of work and worry to prepare (not including last-minute edits from stakeholders with conflicting viewpoints). Moments before the meeting itself, the CEO's assistant calls to say that his previous meeting is running late and asks you to cut your presentation to five minutes. You manage to read out the first line of the executive summary, at which point it becomes clear the CEO just wanted to know whether or not the latest invoice got paid. All that time is wasted because people are too frozen to demand basic clarifying information.

Occasionally, burying your head in the sand can have significant consequences. Barings Bank famously collapsed in 1995 as a result of a single rogue employee losing $1.4 billion through unauthorized trades. Trader Nick Leeson masked his losses and sank deeper and deeper into the red over a number of years, unaware he had eventually exceeded the bank's available trading capital.

Leeson now gives talks about the need for better corporate governance, and a few years ago I heard him speak at a conference. Leeson highlighted multiple reasons for the Barings collapse, including governance limitations. But I remember being struck when at one point he said simply, 'I was too scared to ask for help.'

In a 2016 interview with the Chartered Management Institute, Leeson acknowledged responsibility for what had happened, but he also described why he hesitated to inform a superior of a mistake made by a junior colleague – the mistake that led to him masking a loss for the first time. Leeson said: 'He was not a very approachable person.... He wasn't very good with the local employees and would often belittle them in front of other people.' Not wanting his new colleague to lose her job, Leeson hid the loss-making position in a hidden error account. Over the next few days, the loss 'just got bigger and bigger'.

A further example is that of aerospace company Boeing, where the company's failure to reveal safety issues was cited as a factor behind the crashes of two of its 737 MAX jets in 2018–2019, which led to the death of 346 people. The related 245-page report from the US House Committee for Transportation and Infrastructure makes for sobering reading. In a 2016 survey by Boeing, provided to investigators by a whistleblower, 39% of 'authorized representatives' (Boeing employees to whom the regulator delegated some of its oversight) felt 'undue pressure' to certify the aircraft, and 29% were worried about the consequences if they were to report that pressure. Similarly, at the regulator, the Federal Aviation Administration, 34% of respondents to a draft internal survey gave 'fear of retribution' as one reason for employees failing to report safety issues.

At best, freezing at work wastes time, creates low-level concealment and misses opportunities for doing things better. At worst, the consequences can be catastrophic.

Fawn: we'll get it done

Your manager eyes you with barely suppressed panic across the boardroom table.

'We'll get it done,' she says hastily, interrupting what you're saying to the executive board. Afterwards, she takes you to one side: 'They don't want to hear no,' she says, clearly trying to restrain her impatience. 'Saying no is negative.'

'But the board need to know if something isn't possible,' you say.

'They just want to hear that we'll get it sorted.'

By we, she means you. You sigh and walk back towards your team's desks. JFDI – or 'just f**king do it' – is not normally the precise phrase used, but the meaning is usually pretty clear. You're going to have to cut something essential from your already-stretched plan – and warn people about a lot of late nights ahead.

When speaking about her time on Wall Street, comedian Michelle Wolf once said: 'You just have to get it done. You never say, "I can't," or, "I don't know how." You just get it done.'

If freezing is when people find themselves unable to move at all, fawning is when people try to prevent harm by complying with the source of the threat. Your boss is telling those further up the chain what they want to hear, even when it is unrealistic. Rather than confront the issue, she pushes the problem further down the chain.

I speak to a project manager for a manufacturing firm, who sighs: 'This is my big bugbear. Everyone above you is saying yes, even though it doesn't work. They don't want to know why you can't do it. They are afraid of saying no because they think they will look weak.'

The executive board usually has no idea this is happening: the irony is that they rely on their immediate teams for the right information. The problem comes when they push so hard for results that your boss doesn't feel she can tell them the truth. They probably want accuracy; instead, they are pandered to.

The reward for inspiring fear is not awe, but ignorance. And that's a problem, because if rose-tinted spectacles are dangerous in life generally, they are fatal for a career in senior leadership.

Flee: that's not my role

I begin my research interviews for this book with an open question: What would you most like to change about your workplace? I am startled when, time and time again, the first thing people say is, 'People need to take ownership.' In fact, they say it like this: 'PEOPLE NEED TO TAKE OWNERSHIP!'

Then they breathe out and say, 'Aaahh … I feel better now.'

I thought taking ownership would be *a* thing. I didn't think it would be *the* thing.

Maybe you don't see this – if so, perhaps you work in a small company. In small companies ownership is easier, mainly because you're the only person doing about five roles. Rarely do you need to wonder who's in charge of something. Negotiating a contract? That's you. Training customers? You. Terrifying interview with the national press? That will be you again.

In any medium or large company, responsibilities quickly become a lot more complicated, and this drives a lot of what might politely be called 'sub-optimal behaviour'. People can become Teflon-like in their ability to flee, or evade tasks. One programme director tells me in frustration, 'Everyone wants to be involved in the meetings, to be a voice at the table. But nobody is interested in seeing anything through.'

Why do some people flee their responsibility so determinedly? Sometimes it's down to straightforward confusion. Never underestimate the lack of role clarity in a big company. Or maybe there are rigid processes that mean a team ignores everything except their tiny piece of the jigsaw, because they are simply unable to influence the box that needs ticking before or after them. Generally, though, those who disengage or distance themselves are *seeking safety*. People don't get out of bed in the morning intent on quietly achieving as little as possible. It's more likely that they fear blame.

Of course, people don't openly say that they're afraid of blame. They simply come up with creative ways of being useless. Take the specialists in Being Concerned, who send emails that begin 'I'm concerned about X' but fail to propose any viable solution. This allows them to sit in a future meeting and say, primly, 'I *did* flag my concern about X back in April.'

Then there are those who love saying no to every new idea. They will annoy their colleagues to the point where everyone wants to throw stationery at their head, but they will *never be wrong*.

On the occasions when things do go wrong, some people suddenly assume the role of distant bystanders, and start using phrases like the ones in the following table.

Statement	Meaning
'Apparently ...' or 'I understand that ...'	I am very distant from this problem, so it certainly isn't my fault
'I've just been told that ...'	I've only just heard about this Bad Thing, which clearly stems from a different team
'I'm just an advisor here'	This was my project until five minutes ago, but I've just decided it's all going wrong so wish to distance myself pretty quickly

A friend of mine tells me of the following exchange he once experienced:

> **My friend**: Can you help me with this branding?
> **His colleague**: That's not my role.
> **My friend**: But your job title is branding manager.
> **His colleague** (magnanimously): It's not my job to get involved with actual branding. But I'll be very happy to check it over once you've put it together.

There's a certain logic to it. Claiming that things are not his role is a straightforward way for my friend's colleague to ensure a short and stress-free working day. Even though the limits of his efficacy appear to be inhabiting a desk and possessing a job title, he can't do anything wrong for which he could be blamed.

Finally, there is the phrase 'that's not my problem': a pretty clear sign that people are in a bad place. One customer services director tells me: 'Oh, it happens all the time with one colleague, who can't really cope with her role. She says, "It's not my problem, you're going to have to do it." It is open hostility.'

It has to be said, however, that sometimes the ownership swerve can make a horrible kind of sense. Sometimes the fear of blame is justified, because anyone who volunteers to solve a problem finds that it ends up having their name on it. Months later this enables some other manager, fighting for their own team's share of the bonus pot, to pull a face and say, 'I don't know about Jeff. There was that whole business with The Problem.' In these environments, it is no surprise that people distance themselves from issues as much as possible.

Take the annual budgeting process*: a source of endless amazement and surprise to lots of clever people, even though it falls at precisely the same time each year. Let's imagine for a moment that you are an engineer rushed into providing cost estimates to build various, as-yet-vague new bits of technology. You are given almost zero notice because of the urgent deadline that fell unexpectedly from the sky. *You won't be held to these forecasts,* you are assured. And yet a few months into the new financial year you receive an email from finance asking rather sharply why the cost estimates weren't right. You should be being congratulated on the fact that your estimates even vaguely resembled reality, but instead any discrepancy is perceived as your failure.

You know what? Good engineers can often see that a project is a political hot potato, or that it is going to backfire, but they *take responsibility anyway.* This is because they know it needs doing and no one else is going to step up. The highest-calibre people in any business are likely to be mission-focused types who care about getting the job done, and their biggest bugbear is people who don't take responsibility.

One programme manager tells me in frustration: 'You look around and nobody volunteers to pick up an issue and I say,

---

* Seriously, please take it.

"Well, I'll do it then." I feel this weird sense of responsibility to move things along and do the best for the organization I work for. But it does wear down the people who are willing to put their hand up.'

In his book *Alchemy: The Surprising Power of Ideas That Don't Make Sense*, Rory Sutherland, vice-chairman of advertising agency Ogilvy, writes:

> Although you may think that people instinctively want to make the best possible decision, there is a stronger force that animates business decision-making: the desire not to get blamed or fired.

Self-preservation and making the best decision for the business do not correlate as neatly as one would wish: especially in a corporate environment, longevity in one's career is often more about avoiding errors than it is about making good decisions. Making as few overt decisions as possible may not represent the most interesting or productive path through a business, but it is often the safest.

Of course, self-preservation comes in many guises. Rather than fleeing from ownership, some people do the exact opposite. Take Kevin, who has been at his company for twenty-five years and will proudly tell you that he was employee number 82. Kevin, who remembers the old office and the old logo, has remained employed through endless restructures and changes of technology because he knows every detail of the old Sub-System 2A, which is still embedded in the tech stack despite its obsolete programming language. As the only person who knows about it, Kevin has woven a veil of secrecy and mystique around Sub-System 2A that most of his younger, ambitious bosses simply cannot be bothered to unravel. Long past the point at which he might have been considered for promotion, Kevin is unperturbed that Sub-System 2A is the only thing he will ever be able to do.* The downside, of course, is that Kevin is not incentivized to share his knowledge: if he documents the system, the company may not need him any longer.

While clinging to knowledge seems like the opposite of swerving ownership, the two approaches are actually more similar than one would think because they both involve prioritizing one's own sense of security over the interests of the company. Unfortunately, some colleagues don't see or experience any downside in building themselves a fortress of knowledge – after all, it helps them feel safer.

The amount of insecurity in some companies, and the negative behaviour it inspires, is quite remarkable. The price of fear in an organization lies not so much in what people do, but in what people *don't* do.

- They don't question what needs to be questioned.
- They don't say what needs to be said.
- They don't own what needs to be owned.

Fear stifles productivity and engagement on the quiet, because 'things not done' are generally invisible: people tend to focus on and judge the things that do get done, not those that are silently dropped.

Yet, it is worth fighting for a better environment, because most employees want to get their jobs done. They know that things don't have to be that way. They are incredulous at ownership swerves because they know how great it is when everyone contributes. It is such an underrated facet of working life: working in unison with people you respect, especially on something head-hurtingly challenging, can give you an extraordinary sense of achievement.

---

* Is this you? A bad sign is if your colleagues link your system of choice to your name: e.g. 'Kevin – you know, Sub-System 2A Kevin'.

Reducing fear also shows up in the bottom line: a 2017 Gallup report estimated that it could lead to a 27% reduction in attrition, 40% fewer safety incidents and a 12% increase in productivity.

Creating a safe environment at work is not easy, then, but it's worth it – except there's a massive great elephant in the room. Can organizations ever be considered truly safe places?

The edge of comfort

Are employees always going to feel a certain amount of fear? This is a big question and, clearly, a bit of a problem for anyone seeking to understand and reduce workplace dread. Perhaps you are dreading something specific: an upcoming presentation or awkward conversation. (Ironically, the dread is often worse than the thing itself – when you are in the moment, you will simply get on with it.) Or perhaps the issue is simple: modern employment has insecurity baked in. After all, your presence is conditional on your ongoing strong performance. If you're after unconditional love, don't get a career – get a puppy.

This is not all bad news. That frisson of anxiety you experience before your working week is probably a sign of intellect: it shows you have a reasonable appreciation of whatever responsibility is on your shoulders.*

Fear is often about your immediate leader, or someone above them. Yet, intriguingly, good leaders are not always comfortable to be around. A number of people hesitate while telling me their stories of workplace terror.

'The duality is interesting,' says brand consultant Claire Lowson. She pauses. 'With one former boss, there was a lot of good and bad in the relationship. But I feel like I learned a lot.'

---

* This casts all those colleagues who are permanently serene and unruffled in a new light – they're not somehow better than you, they may be worryingly oblivious.

Spiros Theodossiou, a chief product officer in a fintech firm, tells me over Zoom, 'I once had a really aggressive boss. He was also someone I learned a lot from. He really pushed me to do more.' He adds, 'That's the thing: should a leader provoke enjoyment? Or improvement?'

I reflect upon times I've experienced this myself. One former boss of mine could be enormously intimidating, but he constantly pushed his staff to make better decisions. Most of the fear that my colleagues and I experienced came from a keen desire to be as good as he wanted us to be.

What we are all trying to articulate is that disquieting feeling of fear mixed with respect – that rare alchemy with a leader that pushes you to grow. The Hungarian psychologist Mihaly Csikszentmihalyi said, 'Enjoyment appears at the boundary between boredom and anxiety, when the challenges are just balanced with the person's capacity to act.' You're on the edge of comfort, but you might well be growing as a result.

After all, a good workplace isn't necessarily one where everyone feels snug and cosy. A good workplace also stretches you and gives you things to aim for. Maslow's hierarchy of needs began with basic safety, followed by friendship and belonging, then esteem for oneself and from others. But its pinnacle was 'self-actualization': becoming everything you have the capacity to become. And to achieve that, people occasionally need a push.

The crucial ingredient here is respect, and that is what some leaders forget about. Consider the person in your workplace who is the most intimidating in manner. Do they speak the truth to those above them, even if it is not good news? Do they seek to collaborate rather than to dominate? Do they know how to do the job of those at a lower level if the occasion demands it? Do they constantly seek knowledge? No one is perfect all the time, but these are examples of the things that can build respect. A leader can't just inspire fear and expect to get the same result.

Machiavelli's most famous work, *The Prince*, is best known for one question: is it better to be respected out of love or out of fear? Machiavelli writes, 'It is far safer to be feared than loved.' Yet the key part of his discourse is the statement that comes before: 'If one has to choose between them.'

Fear is certainly the safer choice, but *only if you can't have both*.

Of course, it's easy to say 'People need to feel safe!' This is about as useful as sticking your hand in the air during a brain-storming session and saying, chirpily, 'We need to improve com-munication!' How do you go beyond statements and into action? How do you make it real?

Chapter 3

Telling fear where to go

'Sorry - give me a minute,' says Matt from the front of the room. He pauses and looks down. I get the sense that our small group, clustered round the table of a meeting room, is collectively holding its breath. Matt is not a chatty person. He doesn't tell you how he is at the start of a call. He just focuses on the job, and is so neutral in manner that people sometimes struggle to work out what he really thinks.

Matt clears his throat. 'So, after my grandfather died, I lost my mum as well, just a few months later,' he explains. His voice stops wavering. 'That was hard. But we're all doing OK right now.'

It's 10 a.m. on a Wednesday and I'm in a workshop. But this is not a normal workshop. Colleagues spend time in dedicated sessions – typically a full day – not for training on the latest technology or to learn about leadership, but to get to know each other as people. These particular sessions were initiated after the executive board wanted to make sure that people really lived the company values in their interactions with each other.

Such workshops tend to be quite a departure from a normal working day. I'm usually triple-booked and already grumpy about something else that I have to get done, so I generally bolster my spirits with a large cup of tea and sit sceptically in the corner of the room with a polite smile on my face, waiting for it to be over. But somehow – darn it! – the whole thing works its magic. I get drawn in by the prospect of gaining a new perspective, and by the quiet appeal of considering those around me with a fresh gaze. For these workshops focus on the personal, the anecdotal. For example, the coach will say, 'Share an example of a time when you've failed.' They're not talking about inter-view-question-type failure ('I work too hard!'): they mean real failure. In one workshop I share a time when I cost a previous company a chunk of development budget because I didn't spot a one-line alteration to a 180-page French technical document.* Or the coach will say, 'Draw a line visualizing your life story, with its ups and downs, and then talk it through.' That's what Matt was just doing.

For a few reasons, this kind of initiative needs to be spon-sored by a wise HR department or executive board. Firstly, you need time out of the working day, and secondly, you need a neutral third party in the room to steer proceedings. It doesn't work to book a room and announce you're having a trust work-shop, because it sounds so airy-fairy that cynics (like me) may sniff at it and steer well clear. An independent coach will have the authority to corral everyone. Third-party organizations are a great way to bring valuable structure and perspective to these sessions. Those I participate in are based on a model from the Table Group, Patrick Lencioni's company, which structures ses-sions around the concepts in his noted book *The Five Dysfunc-tions of a Team.*

When it comes down to it, to conquer fear in the workplace, you need trust. For trust, you need mutual understanding. And for mutual understanding, colleagues need to know each other as people.

Many companies are exploring this link between mutual vulnerability and trust. In 2012 a Google team tried to establish the characteristics of high-performing teams through an initi-ative called Project Aristotle. They kept coming up stumped.

---

* This incident gave me a lifelong suspicion of the airy 'FYI' that accompanied its arrival in my inbox.

Why were their results so inconclusive? From the 180 teams that they studied, there appeared to be no meaningful correlation between those that performed best: each had a different composition and did different things. However they cut the data, the Google team were struggling to find similarities.

Their lightbulb moment, described in a 2016 *New York Times* article by Charles Duhigg, was when the team came across the work of Dr Amy Edmondson of Harvard Business School, *the* foremost authority on fear in the workplace. She brought to prominence the concept of 'psychological safety', describing it in a renowned 1999 academic paper as 'a shared belief held by members of a team that the team is safe for interpersonal risk taking'. The key is to create an environment in which colleagues can take risks and speak without fear of being perceived as stupid or being penalized.

For Google, psychological safety turned out to be highly correlated with teams being successful. The teams that thrived created a safe environment for team members because they valued empathy and communication.

Dr Edmondson tells me that, even now, she has to emphasize on Twitter and in podcasts that psychological safety is not about being nice: 'It's not about coddling people in a false sense of security. Rather, it is about a safe environment to challenge or ask questions. It is a foundation stone for constructive conflict, done right.'

Think for a moment about how different a fearful workplace could be if everyone trusted each other. That quiet cascade of dysfunction – the refusal to take ownership, the panic over looking stupid in front of the CEO – would become unnecessary. In its place, you would build a sensible way of spending your week – working alongside a group of people who you know have good intentions.

I'm surprised to find the workshops transformative. My day-to-day relationship with Matt, for example, improves immensely. We always worked together productively, but now and again there was slight tension or moments of incomprehension. Now we have our factual discussions, as usual, but I feel there has been a shift. We're operating from a new base: we understand each other better, and I know we're on the same side.

Management coach Clive Smith says of such workshops: 'Maybe you don't even find common ground. Sometimes it's more about understanding. You may learn someone has a radically different world view to you. But you still understand them better, and that helps future interaction.'

As Charles Duhigg writes of Google's Project Aristotle, 'It's sometimes easy to forget that success is often built on experiences – like emotional interactions and complicated conversations.'

Admitting you're human

Have you ever had a colleague who seems incapable of talking about anything other than work? I recall the following exchange while ordering drinks at the bar next to a US sales director in my first job:

> **Me**: Hi Jasper, how are you?
> **Jasper**: Helen! Name three things you're doing in Q1 to increase revenue.
> **Me**: Jasper, it's 9 p.m. Ask me something normal.

Some leaders never feel able to show anything of themselves in case other people think they're unprofessional.* And yet leaders have a powerful role to play in establishing psychological safety. Trust workshops, however, tend to be mostly between peers. So how do leaders build trust within their teams?

Well, those that do share something of themselves build trust and confidence within the ranks below: *we're all just people*. It's

---

* Or maybe they really do only think about Q1 revenue.

like those companies that allow you to bring pets to work: it's a lot harder to be intimidated by someone once you've seen them hugging their labradoodle puppy.

Rasmus Groth, the former CEO of a start-up I used to work with, used to share what he was reading that week at the foot of his regular newsletter. He later told me that it gave him something to talk about with clients because he felt he was no good at small talk. I loved it: it gave me some great tips for my reading list and showed me that Rasmus stood for something more than just his company.

Leaders who don't have any book recommendations to share can simply admit when they're uncertain. In a conversation for the podcast 'Leadermorphosis', Dr Amy Edmondson told management coach Lisa Gill:

> The most important thing leaders can do is be more open themselves about the challenge that lies ahead. 'We've got this really challenging project. I'm excited about it but I'm nervous also.' When I say something like that as a manager, I just make it so much easier for others to say that too.

In the current era of more remote working, leaders need to be even more open. I speak to Lisa and ask her how leaders can help their teams while working remotely. She tells me: 'Leaders are having a hard time of it. It's harder to build and maintain a positive climate in remote teams because of Zoom fatigue and the lack of spontaneous human connection.'

So what can they do?

'They can let go of the idea that they as leaders need to solve this by coming up with endless creative ideas or "enforced fun",' says Lisa. 'Instead, take a more adult-to-adult approach and enrol people in tackling the challenge together. You could say something like, "I'm hearing – and experiencing myself – that it's really hard to maintain trust and openness in our team right now. What ideas do you have? What would make a difference for you?"'

Leaders can also have a go at saying those three verboten words: 'I don't know'. For a long time it has been drilled into everyone by some unknown, bossy force that you must never admit this. Currently, people who clearly don't know something are obliged to say, in stilted tones, 'I'll just check that with my team and get back to you.'

Stop!

Just say it!

'I don't know!'

The words aren't poison. There is way too much information in the average company – in the average *email* – for everyone to know everything. If leaders start saying 'I don't know', then perhaps everyone can relax a little bit.

Acknowledging failure and moving on from it has a similar fear-reducing effect. Failure is 'I don't know' writ large. You didn't know and then something bad happened as a result. Ugh! Human instinct is to cover it up, but companies now know that's exactly what leads to Bad Things like the 2008 financial crisis. That's why failure is the new trendy buzzword. Failure is the new success! We fail faster than anyone else! At Spotify, some squads of engineers have 'fail walls', where failed projects are shared and learned from. Accounting software firm Intuit reputedly gives a regular Failure Award to the team whose failed project resulted in the most learning.

Those in somewhat less dynamic companies may laugh nervously at this point. They know there is a small, but crucial, distinction between their manager (who has just read a book about an amazing Silicon Valley start-up) announcing that failure is now OK and this *actually being accepted within an organization*. Just ask anyone who's ever had to tell the finance director the revenue forecast has gone down.

What employees know is that when companies talk about embracing failure, few mean *proper* failure. In truth, not all failure is a nice, shiny learning opportunity. Some is just failure, with no upside. Mess up too often – miss your target multiple times or do the same thing wrong more than once – and you will probably find yourself out on your ear. This is evidenced by the kind of failure that the progressive companies celebrate: killing off projects that are not working (which should happen anyway) or rapid-fire trialling of new concepts (which is already an accepted learning approach).

Actually, however, this nuance doesn't matter. Dragging the term 'failure' above the surface, *in whatever context*, still destigmatizes the word for the person who has messed up. The real message about failure is not: 'How great! You learned something.' The true message is: 'If you mess up, please tell us – and tell us quickly.' This is because the mistake is never as bad as the cover-up. This is good for our quest to reduce Sunday night dread, because acknowledging that failure happens removes the shame, which in turn removes the need for blame or concealment. Suddenly, it becomes safer to be accountable for things. Ownership swerves become unnecessary and the general air of panic subsides because people can afford to be nicer to each other. And ... breathe!

The sunny microclimate

What if you're not a leader, or you suspect your organization is not going to invest time in building trust? Well, you could model civility and demonstrate vulnerability yourself and then hope for the best. It's more fun, however, to enlist a core group of colleagues – your immediate team, perhaps – who you suspect also have moments of work-related dread halfway through a Sunday night box-set binge.

What about culture having to come from the top? The executive board certainly tends to sign off on things like those interminable lists of corporate values, but actually the norms that uphold them are more important. Companies might print 'Work smart, play hard' on the lanyard of your security pass, clearly hoping the message will go in via osmosis, but values ultimately come to life through behaviour: how people interact or how decisions are made. Therefore, small actions matter.

Indeed, consider the extent to which any company is a collection of microclimates. Like Venice, where it used to be said that every time you crossed a bridge you would hear the local dialect in a different accent, companies are not as homogeneous as one might think. Different acquisitions, business units and even clusters of desks all produce different microclimates, which means that people from the same company often have radically different workplace experiences. Your immediate team has far more weight in the emotional temperature of your week than a distant and overworked executive board.

So what builds a trusting atmosphere at ground level? One way to foster a sunny microclimate is for the people in a team to make an effort to bolster each other's spirits. This doesn't cost the company any money, and it doesn't require any kind of permission. For example, if you manage to have a face-to-face team meeting, get a bit of paper with everyone's name on top and invite people to each write something that they value about that person. Fold the bits of paper as you go, to conceal the comments, and pass them around. Then give everyone their scroll, with instructions to open it the next time they're having a bad day. I was once in a team where we did this and it was most cheering – to the extent that I still have the bit of paper somewhere.

Maybe that doesn't feel right for your team. Some things work, some things don't. That's fine. Feel free to make something up that works for you. You're looking for anything that encourages goodwill: the glue that is eroded by insecurity and built back up by trust. You do not need to wait for permission. Environmentalist Paul Hawken once said: 'Real change occurs from the bottom up; it occurs person to person, and it almost always occurs in small groups ... then bubbles up and aggregates to larger vectors of change.'

Another idea is to put some focus on the emotional temperature of the team and the individuals within it. Take a look at the work of Joost Minnaar and Pim de Morree, also known as the Corporate Rebels. This duo of spirited Dutchmen have travelled the world visiting companies and meeting individuals who improve or reinvent the world of work. On one visit to Chinese manufacturer Haier they found that employees had created a wall chart to which team members stuck a smiley, neutral or unhappy face before they started work. This allowed team members to share how they were feeling but also helped them carry out their roles more successfully. One factory worker told de Morree:

> If someone doesn't feel well because of a bad situation at home we sometimes decide to send that person home to his family. He or she can focus on their private matter.... We noticed that people that feel bad also made more mistakes. Now we can try to solve both problems at the same time.

An initiative will often work precisely because it is faintly eccentric and distinctive to the team, or because it cements and celebrates norms that are already in place. In 2016, while working for the United Kingdom's Government Digital Service, consultant Giles Turnbull realized that many of the organization's new starters didn't know how the team worked or what kind of culture they were joining. So the team wrote a list, and designer Sonia Turcotte turned it into a poster. The list began with 'It's OK to ...' followed by statements such as 'ask for help' or 'forget things'. It showed that new starters were stepping into a welcoming structure that held certain things dear, such as mutual support. Giles says: 'It occurred to me: maybe it would be helpful to spell out this unofficial stuff up front, on day one. Maybe we just need to say what's ok. To be explicit about the things that those of us who have been here a few years take for granted.'

This is a super-simple way to spread a sense of safety – indeed, it works best if it is done at ground level by employees themselves rather than being a top-down edict.

The ideas that work will often spread. Giles posted his list on the Government Digital Service blog and it promptly went viral. The poster was adopted by other government agencies, health providers and private companies, and was also translated into several other languages. It was even exhibited at the Vienna Biennale in 2017. Since then, further versions have helped organizations make it clear they are empathetic to the challenges of remote working.

Giles tells me, 'In my view, writing a list like this is useful for lots of teams, and lots of organizations. Something simple like this can really help a positive climate grow and thrive.'

Managing conflict

When Nele van Hooste joined the Belgian firm Board of Innovation in 2018, she soon noticed something unexpected: colleagues often sent each other taco emojis. This turned out to be a novel way to express appreciation: a taco emoji meant a pat on the back. The team then began using emojis to take the sting out of feedback: a burger emoji was used when there was good and bad feedback (the meat of the bun denoting the criticism and the burger buns the positive cushioning) and a sushi emoji was used for 'raw', or blunt, feedback.

Agreeing how to manage conflict is well within the reach of every team or working group. Indeed, it's something best done at team level rather than higher up, because each group has a different level of comfort when it comes to conflict. Of course, it is often only when someone changes team that this fact comes to light. Once, when I moved from one team to another, I couldn't believe the level of direct criticism. People were so sharp with each other! No one who was already there seemed to bat an eyelid, though: I had merely stumbled into a different conflict norm.

In contrast, when Olann Kerrison, a VP for a financial firm, moved company he startled his new team with his direct approach. 'When I first started, everyone was surprised by my bluntness,' he tells me. 'I had to explain I didn't expect any artificial politeness and I needed everyone to call each other out. That's what we do now, as a team.'

A conversation on managing conflict typically includes agreeing to criticize ideas but not people, or defining friendly ways to sound the alarm if someone gets too impassioned. In general, you simply want to know roughly what to expect from a dialogue, and crucially, to know that any feedback comes from a good place. Nele van Hooste says of the taco feedback system at Board of Innovation, 'It sounds harsh, but it works precisely because of the context. The sushi, for example, is a symbol to emphasize that feedback is given with nothing but good intentions. The aim is not to hurt anyone, but to point out areas of improvement, for both personal growth and company growth.'

She adds: 'The key lesson here is that small, disarming daily things can help to shape a company culture and help build something bigger.'

What if you have someone who hijacks constructive conflict for their own ends? This can be a challenge. The person may be more senior than you. How will they react if you stand up to them? Holding a discussion about conflict norms is an opportunity for people to share how they feel about conflict, which can help if your colleague merely falls into the category of 'blunt and oblivious'. Even if they're just plain difficult, the fact you've agreed the rules for conflict makes it easier for others to refer back to that agreement and gently point out when things are getting a bit heated.

If all else fails, you may need to be brave. One advertising director tells me that she put her firm's largest account on the line over a client's intimidating approach: 'My client prided herself on "telling it like it is", but one time I heard her shouting at my junior team member from the adjacent room. My team member was in tears. I walked in and said, "I'm stopping this meeting. It is not going ahead while you are speaking to my team in that way." In retrospect, it was quite a risk – it was our biggest account. But we couldn't work like that any longer – it would have brought our business down. After that, the client actually became a lot more civil. She even started calling me to ask my opinion on various things.'

The One Where They're All Friends

Some people, understandably, cringe at the idea of going into a workshop with colleagues and being invited to be vulnerable. There is a quicker and easier way to bond, especially in Anglo-American culture, which involves identifying the nearest pub, putting money behind the bar and letting people figure out the rest for themselves.

That was the approach at QAS, the small London-based software company I worked at after graduating. As the former CEO Simon Worth tells me over bagels and coffee: 'We actively wanted to forge real camaraderie. We funded lots of events. In fact, we often spent money on events instead of taking dividends. It was integral to our culture. When places were limited for a sales or technical conference, everyone would lobby for an invite.'

I remind Simon that if there wasn't an official event, we'd simply invent one. At one point the board even joked about buying the pub next door to the office since so many employees immediately spent their pay cheques in there. When we moved offices in Clapham over one weekend, employees from multiple departments volunteered to spend the day moving computer equipment and setting up new desks in return for some beers in the sunshine afterwards. On another occasion, as part of the company's social committee, I wondered if people might like to start the day with a free breakfast in the office, so some colleagues and I got up early to buy every croissant in the local bakery. The event was so popular that the company decided to fund it on a weekly basis.

Maslow's hierarchy of needs rated friendship and belong-ingness as highly important: third only to safety and shelter. The army has long known this and builds loyalty and affiliation through strong team units, pomp and ceremony. In *The Hidden Power of Social Networks*, authors Rob Cross and Andrew Parker studied more than sixty informal networks in organizations all round the world and concluded that these were where the real work gets done. Invisible networks can obviously cut both ways, but the organizations that can identify and value this intri-cate web are better able to fairly distribute work, understand the real risks of key people leaving, and address crucial gaps in knowledge sharing.

The existence of the invisible organization chart will come as no surprise to anyone who has ever needed something urgently from a grouchy and implacable team, only to feel a palpable sense of relief when their colleague Jamie pipes up, 'Oh, I know Terry. Let me give him a call.' Jamie and Terry have a shared bond after that night at the pub when Terry got drunk and cried about his ex-girlfriend before Jamie eventually put him in an Uber home at 3 a.m. wearing the wrong coat. When it comes to actually getting things done, it's sometimes tempting to throw the official organization chart in the bin.* This is because affilia-tion makes you *want* to help your colleagues. Reluctant defer-ence to a hierarchy is extrinsic motivation, whereas friendships are intrinsic motivation: you want to do a good job for someone you like. Thus, friendship creates tangible value through extra goodwill and extra effort made.

Knowing your colleagues as human beings also helps avoid misunderstandings. If you don't know someone's likely intent, you attribute all kinds of motivations to a curt email ('They're trying to annoy me!') that may or may not be true at all. Once

---

* An alternative assessment of the organization chart, from David Krackhardt and Jeffrey Hanson in the *Harvard Business Review*, is that it represents the skeleton of the organization, while the informal network is its central nervous system.

you know someone, even if the two of you come from different perspectives, you are much less likely to think there's any malice involved. Jen Edwards, a head of product for a media company, puts it well: 'If you know the people you work with, care about them and have mutual accountability, then you don't want to let them down.'*

Companies can't force all this – indeed, one too many forced Zoom happy hours may lead to rebellion and have a negative effect, according to one 2021 study conducted by the University of Sydney. It is the voluntary aspect that is key. Companies can win by simply creating an environment where friendship is possible.

And of course the pub is not the only way – indeed, that method gets frowned upon nowadays because it may exclude those who don't drink, or grumpy working mothers like myself who have to race home. But I would say: *we're only grumpy because we want to be there too*. Don't scrap the drinks, just offer a few alternatives as well: perhaps the occasional lunch or breakfast.

A question: do you have a best friend at work? Since the 1990s, the famous Gallup 'Q12' employee engagement survey has asked people to what extent they agree with this statement. Yet this is described as consistently the most controversial aspect of the venerable survey, with many firms sceptical about its relevance. Annamarie Mann, writing on the Gallup website, defends its inclusion:

> There is one stubborn fact about this element of engagement: It predicts performance.... Gallup research proves that having a best friend at work relates to better business outcomes, including profitability, safety, inventory control, and – most notably – customers' emotional connection and loyalty to the organization. In moderately to highly engaged

---

* For any readers that know Jen, her exact words were, '... then you don't want to behave like a dick'.

organizations, the best friend item, along with recognition and progress, is more predictive of turnover than in less-engaged organizations.

Intriguingly, friendship at work is particularly important for women. Gallup's 'Women in America' study reports that two-thirds of women describe the social aspect of a job as a major reason why they work. Because of the ongoing tension between family and work, the latter needs to feel worth it. Friendship helps tilt the see-saw towards work. Gallup found that women who agreed that they had a best friend at work were less likely to be looking for a new job, more likely to have a positive experience during the day, more likely to take risks that led to innovation, and less likely to report negative experiences such as worry, stress or tiredness.

I realize that some of my closest friendships were formed during my time at QAS: confidants through thick and thin, witnesses at my wedding, allies in the whirlwind of parenting. But is this just me? After all, everyone's workplace experience is super-subjective. Plus, it was my first proper full-time job – do I just have rose-tinted spectacles?

I need to think of a more concrete measure. Eventually, I message the rest of the veteran product team, now scattered across the globe from Hertfordshire to Hawaii. We decide that, as a measure of how well one gets on with one's colleagues, a marriage certificate is fairly hard evidence to refute. After a lot of animated disputes over who got together at what event, I am compelled to call the former CEO and raise the possibility that the board put slightly too much cash behind the bar.

'Did you know there have been at least thirty-five QAS marriages?' I tell Simon, trying to suppress a note of glee.

There's a faintly stunned silence. I add, for good measure, 'And over seventy children?'

'Are you putting this in your book?' Simon manages.

'Yes,' I say.

'Well,' Simon says eventually, 'we did want everyone to see each other as fellow companions on a common journey to profitability.'*

QAS's investment in companionship paid off: staff retention was high and revenue grew year-on-year without exception, from £250,000 in 1992 to £51 million in 2004. In 2004 QAS Ltd was sold to consumer credit firm Experian, making millionaires of its founders – and of a fair few of the employees who sat in the beer garden that Saturday, having helped move all the computer monitors. For every person who thinks that a friendly workplace culture is purely a concern of over-indulged employees who can't hack the hard-edged world of commerce, there is a swathe of research proving, over and over again, that a positive culture shows up in the bottom line. One Glassdoor/MIT study found that investing in the large US firms that won awards in the Glassdoor Best Places to Work survey returned an average of 20.3% per annum, compared with 12.9% for the S&P 500 index as a whole.

Simon is clear on why QAS prioritized building strong connections between team members: 'It wasn't altruism. We needed growth, and for that we needed togetherness. It is the best way to create a successful firm, one that creates value – bottom line profit – year on year.'

Annamarie Mann sums things up nicely in her Gallup article: 'The best friend item is not a soft or oddball question, but one that directly impacts performance. It speaks to why people work – and why they choose to keep working for you.'

---

* At the time, in the early noughties, I remember discussing with the chairman the then-radical trend for HR to frown on workplace relationships. He said, somewhat ruefully, 'Helen, if we fired everyone in this company who was seeing each other, there would be nobody left – except me.'

Combating fear: ideas

Ideas for the top

♦ Are *you* the scary leader? Inspiring fear may have helped you get where you are, but it may be time to drop it. Consider the following:

- Don't shoot the messenger: never make team members feel that raising problems is a problem.
- Be specific about what you want, to avoid people running about behind the scenes. When you say you need 'an update', do you mean a general overview or do you need specific information?
- When did you last get told 'no'? Depending on your seniority, people may not divulge bad news to you unless you ask. A good approach is to finish meetings with, 'Is there anything else I should know?' Try asking the most junior person, not their manager.
- Share something of yourself in emails and, where possible, consider cross-hierarchical social activities, e.g. a regular breakfast with employees.
- Be measured in temperament, particularly with junior staff. They're not paid enough to feel the full force of your wrath. One C-level executive admits, 'I have made the mistake of not switching from fierce to gentle with junior staff. They end up crying, and you feel bad.'
- Having a few favourites may seem harmless. It is not.

- If you're still keen on being a little bit intimidating, get yourself a formidable executive assistant instead. They can be your gatekeeper.

♦ Reconsider your 'difficult-to-manage high potentials'. David Morrison, formerly Australia's Chief of Army, once said, 'the standard you walk past is the standard you accept'. Count the complaints to HR: is the disruption caused by a select few really made up for by their short-term results? Are good people leaving the company rather than continue working with them? Teams who are trying to enable constructive conflict will have a hard time if they don't have your support, because rogue elements will misuse the concept. In their book *No Rules Rules*, Netflix CEO Reed Hastings and INSEAD professor Erin Meyer write about the dangers of the 'brilliant jerk':

> Many may think 'This guy is so brilliant; we can't afford to lose him'. But it does not matter how brilliant your jerk is, if you keep him in the team you cannot benefit from candor.

♦ Try not to recruit psychopaths. This is harder than you might think: you can valiantly ask behavioural questions at interview, but most people know how to come across positively. Have multiple interviewers and compare notes for consistent responses: someone may be adept at telling each interviewer what they want to hear. If possible, speak to applicants' former colleagues: if they laugh nervously and call them a 'character', do more due diligence. Referrals from other colleagues are a good tactic: people generally (though not exclusively – see page 29) recommend candidates who are likely to reflect well on them.

♦ If you do make a hiring mistake, act swiftly, so it does not damage team unity. Your team is likely to be remarkably forgiving of human error – but not of inaction.

♦ As a leader, seek help or briefings from your junior staff: they will like you for it as it shows that you value their perspective and are seeking to learn. And, in turn, all this helps them feel it's OK to not yet know everything.

♦ Ensure HR is sufficiently resourced to allow employees to chat in confidence about toxic behaviour. People will only voice concerns if they feel it is acceptable to do so.

♦ For maximum impact, HR should report directly to the CEO, not to a COO or similar. Management coach Clive Smith tells me, 'The most impressive HR director I ever worked with was involved in finance, sales, marketing – everything. HR can influence the overall agenda.'

♦ Ensure objectives take into account how people get their results as well as the results themselves.

♦ As well as modelling expected behaviour, organizations can spell it out. 'We train new team members on culture,' says Martina King, CEO of the artificial intelligence company FeatureSpace. Similarly, Airbnb has a week-long onboarding process that emphasizes the company's values and ways of working. Have a senior leader deliver the training to show that it matters.

♦ In non-sales environments, measure people against objective goals by all means, but *not against each other*. For example, set employees targets to beat their own previous efforts.

♦ If you are office-based, don't be too stern about the hot-desking policy, which can unwittingly destroy clusters of affinity.

♦ Be sure to identify 'knowledge is power' people: these staff members represent operational risks. Insecure colleagues need to know there's a place for them even if they sacrifice their specialist knowledge. Advertising internal promotions or sideways moves more heavily can help reassure people.

♦ Track your retention rate. If people are leaving from the same team or group, find out why. Ask HR to conduct exit interviews for all leavers. Not only is this a courteous act that shows you are listening, but you are bound to receive nuggets of insight.

♦ Conversely, to see an organization through fresh eyes, take advantage of the perspectives of the not-yet-indoctrinated: ask new starters to write an 'astonishment report' of what they've observed in their first ninety days. What do they find surprising or new about the business – be it processes or culture?

Ideas for you

♦ If you have a particularly bad bout of Sunday night dread, ask yourself what is the worst thing that could happen. Would that outcome still matter in five years' time? The answer is usually no. (Obviously there are times where this doesn't work. 'Apply your five-year rule!' my husband said optimistically, as I sobbed in his arms after the 2016 result of the Brexit referendum. 'BUT IT WILL STILL MATTER IN FIVE YEARS!' I said.)

♦ The longer the break, the greater the dread upon returning to work: you will feel far worse after a week off than after a normal weekend. It shouldn't be this way, but it is. Simply being aware of this sometimes helps you feel better.

♦ Face your fear. Whatever is causing your dread, try to tackle it as early as possible on Monday morning. This is not a tough-love approach but a gift to yourself, precisely because the dread of the thing is usually worse than the thing itself.

♦ If you are stuck with an obstructive or difficult colleague, the best approach is often, counterintuitively, to be kind and show you recognize their strengths, because their behaviour so often comes from a place of insecurity.

♦ For really toxic, shouty people, you may have to 'think big picture'. Trust that these people are a short-term irritation, soon to be pushed out or propelled elsewhere by their conviction in their own brilliance. At some point the person troubling you will be a minor footnote in the story of your life.

♦ Be factual with those who are more senior than you, even if it's not good news. If nothing else, the near-term terror of sharing bad news is less scary than the lurking dread of a cover-up.

♦ Sometimes there are simply so many people in a company that there is confusion over role scope. A director in a fintech firm tells me: 'People must own something and drive it. Overlap in roles kills culture. If there's cross-over then either everyone steps back and things fall through the gap, or it creates conflict.' Do the boring stuff: have a job specification for each role or knock up a quick spreadsheet that confirms who is responsible for what.

♦ Where possible, organize informal social events. A low-cost, inclusive idea for those based in an office is a 'multicultural food' day, where everyone brings in a lunch or dinner dish connected to their nationality.* If some of the team is working remotely, ask them what they want: don't try to enforce yet another quiz.

---

* This was the brainchild of Leyla Kazim, now a presenter for BBC Radio 4's 'The Food Programme', when we used to sit next to each other at work. Unsurprisingly, her contributions were amazing.

♦ Make sure that you and your colleagues include a photo in your email profile so that others are not interacting with a blank avatar. Ask the same of new teams or colleagues. This is particularly important if teams are working remotely.

♦ New to an organization? One approach is to build rapport with senior members of staff before you've had time to be terrified by their fearsome reputations. In his first week as a graduate intern, my ex-colleague Pratik Choudary went to the company's CEO and asked to shadow him for the day. The CEO, despite probably being startled by his chutzpah, said yes – and remarked that that is what he would have done in his position. Rapport built!

♦ Sometimes a bonded team looks like a great success, but it has chosen the wrong glue: the shared dislike of a different team. Try really hard not to bond your team in this way. And if it's too late, be brave: do what you least feel like doing and talk more often with that other team, not about what you need but about why you need it. If your goal involves revenue, emphasize this. Non-revenue-generating teams are often keen to show their value in monetary terms and your revenue goal might help them prove their worth. Alternatively, take a deep breath and schedule a shared activity of some sort. It's harder to demonize people once you know them.

♦ Get ownership-swervers and those who are resistant to change 'out there' to meet customers. Understanding the needs of real customers has three big advantages: it shocks people out of their negative groove; it is motivating to meet the needs of real people; and, most importantly, it provides confidence when making decisions. 'I know our customers value X, so that's what we should prioritize.'

♦ If rudeness spreads, so can civility. In one research study led by Adam Grant and Francesca Gino, being thanked for their help made participants more than twice as likely to assist someone else because it increased their feelings of social worth.

PART II
FOCUS

Chapter 4

Data overload

Think of a book or film that you particularly like. What happens in it?

A fair bet is that the hero or heroine is seeking something they really want or have been compelled to achieve. It's one of the rules of fiction and screenplay: give your protagonist a goal, then chuck a whole load of barriers and obstacles in their path. (For extra drama, make the obstacles harder as they go along.) The writer and director George Abbott summed it up as follows: 'In the first act, your hero gets stuck in a tree. In the second act, you throw stones at him. In the third act, you get him out of the tree.'

This is great in film and fiction, because you get to experience your hero grappling with impossible tasks while you happily eat chocolate from the comfort of your sofa. But wouldn't it be nice if the working week didn't resemble the same epic struggle to get things done?

In part I of the book we looked at fear, insecurity and its ripple effects. This part deals with focus – or, more accurately, the loss of focus – at work: those situations when work feels like wading through mud. 'Why is everything so slow and complicated?' you yell in frustration halfway through a call (hopefully while on mute), chucking crumpled-up bits of paper at the nearest wall.

Freud famously said, 'Love and work are the cornerstones of our humanity.' He didn't mean work in the sense of a diary crammed with compliance training or potentially ominous meetings innocently entitled 'Quick catch up'; he meant that people innately want a sense of purpose and to be productive.

This is such an infuriating contradiction of working life: you are hired to do something you are reasonably excited by, only to find you have to fight through masses of emails, paperwork or endless swerves in priority in order to achieve it. These are not even proper dramatic, film-type obstacles, you think in disgust. It is not as if you're scaling a cliff face or outwitting some terrorists in a siege. You are not being rewarded with a passionate clinch with someone good looking, or even valiantly coming out stronger at the other end. These are just boring, company-made obstacles.

It's like a giant cosmic joke – or perhaps, unbeknownst to you, you are featuring in a hit screenplay.

Email: the time-suck

In *Sapiens,* his sweeping history of humankind, Yuval Noah Harari describes the agricultural revolution as 'history's biggest fraud'. Beginning around 12,000 years ago, the process of moving from a nomadic lifestyle to an agrarian one has been presented by historians as a time of great progress for humanity. But while it certainly did enable population growth, it also created conflict over land, impoverished a once-varied diet and made populations more vulnerable to famine from crop failure. All this happened in such small increments, though, that no one really noticed the shift. And even if they had observed it, the shift was irreversible: populations swiftly grew too big to return to their old, nomadic ways.

Harari asks, 'Why did people make such a fateful miscalculation? For the same reason that people throughout history have miscalculated. People were unable to fathom the full consequences of their decisions.'

The concept of unintended consequences is what I think about whenever I open my email inbox. How did we get into this ungodly tangle: being bombarded with hundreds of competing demands on our time? Visualize, for a moment, the email threads between everyone who works at your company, to-ing and fro-ing on every topic under the sun. In your case, they include urgent requests from your manager that you may not even spot amidst the deluge. We humans welcomed email with out-stretched arms, thrilled by its speed and the little pinging noise from a new message, and now we cannot wind back the clock.

As it is a norm to have far more work than is manageable, your dread of work may be simple exhaustion at the thought of the volume of tasks ahead. You no doubt know the 'false busyness' of a day spent answering emails as if you are volleying tennis balls while your own to-do list becomes dust. Meanwhile, your inbox is useless at congratulating you on what you have done that day. Tick! You think, as you smugly hit reply on some-thing. Your spirits quickly fade, though, as you look at the rest of your inbox: a dispiriting list of all the things you have, as yet, failed to achieve. Every unanswered message is an unmet obli-gation, a small debt.

Writing in the *Harvard Business Review*, academics Rob Cross, Reb Rebele and Adam Grant report that people spend around 80% of their work time answering email, in meetings or on the phone. Communication systems such as Slack, Yammer, Micro-soft Teams and so on offer alternative ways to communicate, but they tend to be used *as well*, not instead of email. So while they can improve information flow, they also increase the num-ber of possible channels. (Note: techies in particular get really passionate about their favourite systems, so you also constantly lose time listening to Grumpy Dave, a Slack devotee, complain-ing about your organization's choice of Microsoft Teams.)

As Grumpy Dave will quickly tell you, it isn't necessarily the most senior who are drawn into the largest number of interac-tions. Rob Cross, Reb Rebele and Adam Grant found that, in the 300 organizations they researched, tasks were distributed in a highly uneven manner. Just 3–5% of staff members contributed

20–35% of added value. These people could be anywhere in an organization chart, but are often individual contributors. This leads to a spiral effect: the more helpful and valuable people are, the more sought after they are, and the more their workload grows – in both volume and variety of tasks. And yet this can often go unseen by those higher up the seniority ladder. This means that the strongest performers in an organization may be both overworked and simultaneously undervalued by their own managers, who simply don't see the work they do. Cross states: 'When we use network analysis to identify the strongest collaborators in organizations, leaders are typically surprised by at least half the names on their lists.'

Of course, this assumes your colleagues' messages are good natured – that email is a problem of volume alone. What about when the communication itself feels like an obstacle?

Energy vampires

In the comedy TV show *What We Do In the Shadows*, a group of vampires share a house in modern-day Staten Island. Most of them are traditionally recognizable vampiric types, with dark, gothic clothes and capes. One, however, wears the garb and mild-mannered countenance of an average cubicle-dwelling office worker. This is Colin Robinson, and he is an energy vampire. Energy vampires drain energy from their co-workers. In Colin's case, he does so by boring them with anecdotes about different types of car wash.

Unfortunately, many of us encounter a Colin in our day-to-day work. They obstruct and irritate in a low-level, pervasive way – less hand grenade, more paper cut. I find it highly cheering when I hear the wide array of terms that people use to describe these colleagues. 'Oh! You mean dementors!' says one really quite senior executive, having merrily named them after the Azkaban prison guards that suck positive thoughts from your brain in the *Harry Potter* books. Rob Cross and Andrew Parker, authors of *The Hidden Power of Social Networks*, describe these individuals as 'de-energizers'.

Email is an ideal tool for this kind of colleague, providing an irrefutable record ideal for, at best, ambiguous shorthand and, at worst, back-covering and veiled pomposity. See the following table for some prime examples.

What the energy vampire writes	What they actually mean
As you're aware ... *Or* As discussed ...	I've never mentioned this before and we both know it.
Apparently X is finished ...	I am broadcasting my deep suspicion about whether X is finished, while my tone remains beyond reproach.
I did CC you back in April	I am outraged that you failed to spot the action point hidden halfway through that ten-page email I sent.
Thoughts?	I want to know exactly what you think even though I couldn't even be bothered to write you a full sentence.
FYI	Ignore this and delete it, it's not that important. *Or ...* Action immediately. Ignore at your peril!
This looks like one for you, Bob!	I hate you, Bob, and I always have done.

Do not forget the CC-ers and the escalators. The CC-er includes everyone in their email, including someone they once met in the canteen. The escalator, meanwhile, is the CC-er's evil twin. They send an indignant email to everyone three levels above you in order to solicit a reply to the email they sent you five minutes ago, while you were in a meeting. One C-level executive tells me wryly: 'One time I was in a thread with our South American office and someone cc-d in someone new with the words, "Jesus now in copy." I thought for a second, "Wow – now there's an escalation."'

Sometimes the issue is long-standing, unsolvable or, indeed, already resolved. This does not trouble the escalator, who may

WHY YOU DREAD WORK

send multiple, separate threads. This allows *lots* of different people at many different levels – notably, your boss and the escalator's boss – to all become very indignant with each other, when all the escalator needed to do was pick up the phone or, if possible, walk over to your desk and ask you their question.

You may have heard of the disinhibition effect, whereby the fact that communication is online allows people to say things they wouldn't say 'in real life'. Work email is much less shouty than online trolling – there are fewer capital letters, fewer violent insults and, mercifully, better spelling – but it still prompts some people to communicate in a way that they would never contemplate if they were addressing another human being face to face.

You may also observe that irritating emails often come from someone with just enough power to mess up your day. They display a strange blend of both pettiness and pomposity:

'No, you didn't ask before 3 p.m.'

'No, you need to get sign-off from your manager.'

Professor Nathanael Fast of the University of Southern California has examined this phenomenon in a research study titled 'The destructive nature of power without status'. Fast explains that sometimes power and status are correlated, but in many jobs they are not. There are roles – such as nightclub bouncer, airport security worker or administrative worker in a benefits agency – in which people have power but also relatively low status in the eyes of others. Fast and his fellow researchers found that those with power but low status were more likely to demean others. They theorized that having low status makes you feel aggrieved, while having power frees you to act upon those feelings: a dangerous combination. In their study, Fast and his team proposed that those with low status may demean others 'not because they were powerful per se but because, despite their power, they felt a lack of respect and admiration'. Meanwhile you, the person trying to get something out of them, wonders why they're being such a pain.

All these energy-sapping interactions have a disproportionate impact. It may be one interaction out of several hundred but it is so annoying that it sticks in your mind and ripples through to other parts of your day. In one research study, 80% of employees lost work time worrying about incidents of workplace rudeness. A 2020 study by researchers at the University of Illinois even found a correlation between receiving a rude email and having trouble sleeping. And incivility tends to spread, so it's a negative spiral. Before you know it, *you* could be the energy vampire. Aagh!

Calls and coffee and Zoom: oh my!

Email is not the only source of dread in the workplace. You probably often find your working day booked solid with meetings, including over lunch. Sometimes it is an all-day workshop, but more often the culprit is a treacherous run of half-hour meetings, each discussing something totally different and requiring thought and preparation in advance. Context switching, or the requirement to think about lots of different subjects one after the other, can be an invigorating challenge or a nightmarish joke, depending on how you're feeling. Charlotte Webb, a chief fundraising officer for a charity in Australia, tells me, 'It's a relentless mental juggle, switching your brain from strategic work one minute, to working with a team member to shape a proposal.' Meanwhile, a study reported by the Amerian Psychological Association found that task switching can incur costs of as much as 40% of productivity.

One *Harvard Business Review* article reports that white-collar workers spend an average of just under twenty-three hours per week in meetings. The equivalent figure for the 1960s was less than ten hours. Meanwhile, a 2018 UK Working Lives report from the Chartered Institute of Personnel and Development (CIPD) found that 30% of workers said their workload was unmanageable. The technical director of a US software engineering firm tells me a typical story: 'I average nine meetings a day in a nine-hour day. It's so soul destroying. I have so little time with my team.'

Surely, by now, meetings deserve their own collective noun? A migraine of meetings? A tedium of meetings? At least with email you can hit the delete key with gleeful abandon. It's harder to get out of meetings and calls, though, which is tough to swallow when most conference calls go something like this:

[Beep]

Organizer: Hello there, who's on the line?

Dave: It's Dave.

Organizer: Hi Dave.

[Beep]

Organizer: Hello, who just joined?

Jeff: It's Jeff.

Organizer: Hi Jeff. Wow, what time is it where you are? [It is 5 a.m. where Jeff is. Jeff is American. This is what Americans do.] OK, it's four minutes past ... we'll give the others a few minutes ... no, actually, let's get started. I'll just share my screen.

[Five minutes of actual meeting]

[Loud crackle]

Organizer: If you're not speaking, please can you go on mute?

[Unexpected silence]

Organizer: Joanne, are you on mute?

Joanne: Sorry, I was on mute.

[Beep]

Joanne: Sorry, the line dropped and I had to dial back in.

Organizer: We're out of time! I'll rebook as soon as I can get this group together. I think it'll be in about two weeks?

Even productive meetings generate more and more work without any corresponding increase in the amount of time available to actually achieve anything. More stressful – or faintly hilarious, depending on how hysterical you are feeling – is the new trend for enthusiastically double-booking or even triple-booking people when it's perfectly obvious from their diary that they're not free. When someone is swearing colourfully at their screen or you can see their frown lines even over a video call, they have usually just received yet another meeting request that blissfully ignores their prior commitments. The more you are paid to be proactive and add value, the more your diary is likely to be jammed with stultifying levels of activity.

For those working remotely, the most useful bit of a meeting has disappeared. By the useful bit, I mean the five seconds right at the end where people pick up their coffee cups and prepare to run to the next meeting. In a face-to-face environment, this is when the real business of the meeting is normally concluded and any confusion is ironed out. In a world of video calls, you just hang up and dial straight into the next one. When does anyone get any time to think?

'At night,' groans the head of a network security team. He sounds muffled down the phone, as if his head is in his hands. 'The only time I have to actually do work is in my free time, once the children have gone to bed.'

Everyone is spread too thinly to focus. You don't have time to make good decisions. You don't have time to think in between meetings. You barely have time to grab lunch. And then you remember you've still got admin to do.

Infernal processes

In 1320 Dante Alighieri wrote his masterpiece *Inferno*: a vivid, medieval depiction of hell. He wrote of the deepest sins of the soul and the darkest punishments that the devil could inflict upon humanity. It is perhaps fortunate that he never had to log in to an HR recruitment system to get a job vacancy approved.

We all know the story: a company champions fast action and independent thinking but requires ten sign-offs and a long-lost thirteen-digit password (with at least one special character) before you can get a new laptop. I ask a friend of mine if he's experienced any annoying internal processes. He flinches. 'Every procurement and HR system ever. Too many. I try to blank them out.'

Of course, companies need some structure and uniformity. Yet companies everywhere tie themselves up in knots with unwieldy processes and systems. Sometimes the process appears to matter more than the thing it is trying to achieve. I hear of one example where it took so long to approve a vacancy that, by the time they were given permission to hire, the recruiting manager themselves had left. Another common bugbear is setting up a new payee in a procurement system. A programme manager tells me: 'It took someone in my team six months to get a supplier set up on our system. The supplier, a household name, was threatening to withdraw from the agreement that had taken two years to set up because we weren't paying them.'

Often the admin is sold to you as 'self-service', which translates as, 'We got rid of the team that used to do this for you.' Often, the work hasn't disappeared, it has simply been pushed in a slightly different form onto the company's broader pool of employees, who are in some cases paid substantially more than the team who used to do it. All this hits the people in the middle of an organization, who are typically overscheduled but not senior enough to merit any administrative support. A partnership manager tells me: 'We manage our meetings and calls, sort out rooms and lunches, book and approve travel, do our expenses. The list goes on. I'm paid to focus on the big-picture stuff, yet I spend all my time on admin.'

Companies are missing a trick here: administrative assistants are much cheaper than a mid-tier manager's time, but there's no way the busiest people will get one because assistants are correlated to status, not workload.

Now and again the bureaucracy becomes borderline comedic. I interview one person who tells me she is signed off sick with anxiety and burnout. I find myself thinking of her and hoping her scheduled return went smoothly. I message her: 'How did it all go this morning?' She replies: 'I've had to come home again because IT had logged me off all the systems, even though they knew I was due back today. They've said it will be ten days to get my access restored.'

The 24/7 work week

Unsurprisingly, all this overload massively impacts how you feel about your working week, because it leaves you struggling to focus on the goals you were hired to accomplish. Meanwhile, too much process stifles autonomy, slowing people down and demotivating them as well, for good measure. Data overload also contributes to abrasiveness, because it makes people stressed and frustrated: they want to accomplish their objectives but when are they going to get them done? Dread of any sort so often stems from a lack of control.

At its worst, data overload creates a sense of paralysis – it can feel as if there is no point trying. There appear to be so many emails, meetings and administrative processes to wade through that people feel they cannot make a dent in their workload. This is what propels people into a self-medicating day off. Colleagues rarely want to call in sick: they don't want to get behind or cause more work for other people. The biggest driver for a sick day is feeling like a day's work simply won't make much difference either way: the deluge will just keep coming.

Everyone feels like they need more time, and it has proven impossible to get this space into the standard working day. Companies have got partway through this line of thinking and reached a troubling conclusion. 'The answer is "work–life integration",' they say airily. 'We don't talk about "work–life balance" any more. It's "life meets work!" We don't encourage an *artificial divide*.'

This sounds great on the surface. After all, people like flexibility. It allows parents to attend parents' evenings,* enables the finance director to go on his Lycra-clad lunchtime run, and so on. And the coronavirus pandemic has introduced many companies all over the world to the validity of remote working. The trouble is that alongside the idyll of flexibility come creeping new norms. Just as we sleepwalked into the problems related to email, we are sleepwalking into an 'always-on' culture, where we dissolve all boundaries between work and home.

I once had an interview with a well-known Big Tech firm and asked how it would work from London with a Silicon Valley HQ. 'How would you feel,' I probed, 'if I started at 7.45 a.m. but left at 5 p.m. to collect my children from the childminder by 6 p.m.?' The recruiter cheerily assured me it wouldn't be a problem: 'Oh, LOTS of people take a break around that time of the day! You just log on again at about 9 p.m.'

A 2017 Kantar Futures/American Express study found that 50% of millennials and 40% of Gen-Xers felt pressure to be available for their employers 24/7. You no doubt know Parkinson's Law, coined way back in 1955: that work expands to fill the time available for its completion. The trouble is that expectations also expand to fill the time available. And technology now allows us to work at any time, and from anywhere. What is more, with colleagues in different time zones, someone is always waking up just as you are logging off. One 2021 study reported in *The Guardian* found that, when working from home, UK and US employees spend an extra two hours *per day* at their computer. They may be conscious that many of their apps and tools allow their employer to see whether they are actively working or not. Are these employees any better off than the person who used to work late in the office after hours – the one who had to wave his arms every five minutes so that the lights wouldn't go out, and whom the cleaner had to vacuum around?

------

* Which, despite the name, always seem to be held mid afternoon.

Wherever they are based, give employees a notional twenty-four hours a day to do their jobs, in a competitive and insecure environment, and what you actually give them are voluntary shackles – ones that they never fully cast off.

If this sounds ridiculous, I know plenty of people for whom holidays are only ever a geographical break and not a mental one: they make sure they are contactable throughout, whether they're at home or on a Greek island. I was once at a team dinner with a visiting manager who proudly told the assembled company that a colleague had taken calls during her own sister's wedding on an idyllic beach in order to close a deal. This was a tale of her extreme dedication to her job. I bit my lip, thinking: she can never get that moment back.

In recent years it has become fashionable for companies to give their employees unlimited holidays. Take what you need, is the message. Yet the result, typically, is that employees take *fewer* days off. People become uncertain about how much they dare take, and not taking holiday can become a kind of virtue signalling. Mathias Meyer, former CEO and cofounder of Travis CI, has written about why his company eventually retracted the policy: 'They [employees] don't want to seem like that person who's taking the most vacation days. It's a race to the bottom.'

Everyone I know works hard. We all deserve to throw ourselves wholeheartedly into work we love, but we all deserve to live, too. Otherwise the modern career is a type of self-induced slavery – something that would have been incomprehensible to the workers of a hundred years ago, when there was a clear exchange of hours of labour for money. Indeed, the workers of just twenty years ago would have found all of this startling. In my first company, an ambitious* colleague used to rig his email program to auto-send his emails in the small hours, so people would think he was highly dedicated and working late. If he

---

* OK, slightly irritating.

rigged up the same system now, no one would bat an eyelid: half of us are still online anyway.

France was the first country to recognize the downside of this cultural shift when, in 2017, it created a law that protects French workers' 'right to disconnect'. Companies with fifty or more staff are obliged to set rules regarding the hours when employees should not send or answer emails, with the goal of protecting private time. In January 2021 an EU resolution was passed calling for the law to be replicated across Europe. But it hasn't been plain sailing. A major survey in France in 2021 reported that 78% of respondents didn't believe their company had properly implemented the 2017 law.

The flow of tasks is so relentless that our entire lives are being given over to work. No one is holding us at gunpoint: we are handing ourselves over, unbidden. But what price are we paying? It turns out that the connection between downtime and creative thought is only just beginning to be understood.

Chapter 5

What we can learn from freestyle rap

In 2012, deep in the research lab of the US National Institute on Deafness and Other Communication Disorders in Maryland, twelve freestyle rap artists underwent an unusual experience. While in the institute's magnetic resonance imaging (MRI) scanner they were asked to perform freestyle rap: that is, to perform using lyrics that they came up with on the spot rather than using material they already knew.

'It's not a very natural environment,' neuroscientist Allen Braun told The Scientist. 'But they did quite well, and no one really complained.'

In examining the rappers, Braun and his team were looking for the brain sequences involved in creativity. They found that the dorsolateral prefrontal cortex – the part of the brain responsible for regulating other brain functions – showed lower activity during freestyle rap than during a conventional performance. In other words, the areas of the brain responsible for focused thought were being dialled down. It appeared that creativity didn't come from focusing directly and intently on a problem or challenge. The most creative thought in fact required an *absence* of conscious focus, allowing a stream of uncensored creativity that was generated not entirely consciously. This may help explain why so many creative types say they can't fully explain how they create their work. It just ... comes from within them.

While it would be highly ill advised of me to attempt any freestyle rap, I know that I add most value when I come up with creative ideas and solutions, not when I'm just reacting to information. Often, these ideas come out of nowhere, while I'm doing something else. And that isn't unusual: one multinational study by the cognitive scientist Scott Barry Kaufman found that 72% of people reported having their best ideas in the shower. Some even reported having more creative inspiration in the shower than they did at work. In the shower you're (usually) alone and you tend to disengage your brain, and this freedom from active thought allows your subconscious to come to the fore. As Kaufman states, 'The relaxing, solitary, and non-judgmental shower environment may afford creative thinking by allowing the mind to wander freely, and causing people to be more open to their inner stream of consciousness and daydreams.'

Unfortunately, if you jump into the shower and stand, poised, ready to receive your day's inspiration, you're likely to emerge soggy but disappointed. The recent marketing of waterproof 'shower notepads' may be missing the point, because it is only in relaxing and unhinging one's mind that the subconscious genuinely gets to work. Sleep is widely understood to perform a similar function, which is why sleeping on a problem will often genuinely help you wake up with fresh answers.

What does this mean for you? It means one crucial thing: you *need* those moments of 'nothing'. This means *proper* nothing, preferably in silence. Both at work and at home, switch off and have times when your brain is quiet and not stimulated by external information – or even by any conscious attempt to focus.

Our busy diaries may make it seem like we're being productive, but our brainpower is not being used to its full potential. What is missing is simple: the lost pulse of our own inspiration. We must preserve the gaps between conscious activity because, counterintuitively, that is when the ideas will come.

Listening to Seneca

Apart from insisting on headspace, and possibly taking longer showers, how can we get past data overload?

We could do worse than take our lead from the philosopher Seneca, who cottoned on to this issue no less than 2,000 years ago. He wrote:

> No one pursuit can be successfully followed by a man who is busied with many things. The mind, when its interests are divided, takes in nothing very deeply.

Despite all our protestations about technology being at fault, humans have felt the perils of divided attention for at least two millennia. We cannot solely blame technology, because our splendid human curiosity, drive and aptitude for variety makes us our own worst enemies. We can happily initiate 'no-meeting Wednesdays' (Facebook does that) or 'no-tedium Tuesdays' (that's one I just made up), but we can't control the tide. People are always going to send messages. People are always going to book meetings. At the risk of sounding like a cheesy quotation you might find on Instagram, we can't change the thing itself, we can only change how we react to it.

There will always be too much work: you simply have to learn to *leave some expectations unmet*. Modern working life doesn't allow you the luxury of everyone being happy with you. You have to make your peace with this uncomfortable fact, and then prioritize ruthlessly. Look at what you need to achieve today and focus on that. Write your to-do list on a Post-It, ideally the night before, and stick it somewhere visible. You won't get any more than that done anyway.*

For email, the principle of Schrödinger's inbox may be useful. That is, if you don't see your messages, then they're both there

---

* Resist the temptation to cheat by using tiny writing.

and not there: both realities exist. Don't look at your inbox until 10 a.m., if you can manage it. You'll be surprised how much more in control this makes you feel. This is because you will have just done all the things you're being chased for, and can therefore respond not with defensiveness but with airy efficiency.

You may also find there is a radical difference between what you can achieve with one hour of your time in the morning and what you might achieve with the same amount of time at, say, 3 p.m. Really focus on and get to know your productive times of day rather than forcing yourself through your low-energy hours. If you are at your best in the morning, do the most crucial thing first. Save admin or tasks that require minimal thought for your moments of flagging energy in the mid afternoon.

Meanwhile, be strict about video calls and meetings. Firstly, does it have to be a meeting? If it can be resolved more quickly with an email, then decline. Yes, we all know face to face is better, but life is short. Prioritize face to face for new acquaintances, but if the meeting is with someone you've worked with for two years, you can probably afford to exchange a swift message. Secondly, do *you* need to be there? Perhaps you could only attend for part of the slot, if need be? Thirdly, can the meeting be shortened? You can buy time to tackle other things on your to-do list by setting up forty-five minute meetings instead of hour-long ones. 'I never do a full hour,' says chief fundraising officer Charlotte Webb. 'Anything that needs to be discussed can be discussed in forty-five minutes. I tried thirty, but forty-five is best.'

Meanwhile, Nick Jenkins, director of Australian software engineering firm Mechanical Rock, has a good way to tackle context switching. He calls his team's technique 'the check-in'. He says: 'If someone joins a meeting and is clearly still preoccupied by the previous one, we ask them to briefly articulate what their previous meeting was about. It helps them acknowledge their previous topic, then they can park it and really be present.'

If, despite your best efforts, you're stuck in a long meeting, always establish at the start what outcome everyone needs from it so it doesn't turn into a lovely chat with no clear resolution at the end. Keep an eye on the time. One former colleague sometimes kept her agenda on track by sounding a small toy horn if anyone veered off topic or spoke for too long.*

Or, show people the money – literally. One contractor tells me: 'At one place, I put up a live counter of how much the meeting was costing, based on salaries and my day rate. That certainly focused people.'

If it comes to it, you can always use unavoidable meetings to give you headspace. Enter meetings with a secondary goal in mind, such as a difficult work issue that you need to think about. This is not being rude: it is optimizing the time available. And anyway, no one can read your mind.

Once you put on your own oxygen mask, you can start helping others. Try discussing email and its conventions with your team or project group. What do they want to see? And what would they really like to banish? If nothing else, it will be cathartic, as people realize they're not alone in their challenges. Discuss what you all intend when you write certain things, and ideally agree a shorthand that means the same thing to everybody. Here are a few practical examples that have been agreed on by previous teams or project groups that I've participated in.

- If there's an action or deadline, everyone should feel free to state it in the first line of their email, or even in the subject line. Agree together that you are not being rude: this is designed to display the most important information first.
- Never just write 'FYI' if action is needed from the recipient
- Do not write 'Dear all' if you need any kind of answer, because this leaves no one in particular accountable for a response. Decide on a few primary recipients in the 'To' field and address them by name.

---

* This was highly effective, although I should note the unwelcome side effect of everyone nursing murderous thoughts towards her.

- Use plain English.
- Never write something in an email that you wouldn't say to someone face to face.
- Rather than giving a flat 'no', get into the mindset of answering requests with 'yes, if ...'. In a rational world it should make no difference, but the brain registers negatives much more strongly than positives, and this smooths a lot of tricky email interactions.
- To avoid others escalating, which invariably wastes time, always volunteer some basic empathy. Begin with, 'I understand how important this is' or similar. Often what annoys people is not the message itself but the fact they feel their respondent doesn't care.
- Don't write in the order you think ('Last night I was thinking about ...'), write in the order the recipient needs the information ('I want to propose a change to X'). Frontload the actions and the deadlines. Background context can go at the end.

Also, be concise. Try channelling the alleged 1862 telegram exchange between the French novelist Victor Hugo and his publisher. Hugo was keen to know how his book *Les Misérables* had been received, but he had to pay for telegrams by the character. So he sent his publisher a single question mark. In reply he received a similarly brief response: a single exclamation mark.

The most important key to a better relationship with email is simple: always presume good intent. People rarely set out to be energy vampires; they probably just got bitten themselves at some point.

Finally, we must not forget that the workplace will never stop making demands of our time. Take the wise words of Larry Kanarek, Sheryl Sandberg's former boss at McKinsey & Company. Sandberg recounts in her book *Lean In* that Larry would hold resignation interviews with burned-out people, only to find they all still had unused holiday leave. Sandberg writes of his reaction, 'Larry implored us to exert more control over our careers. He said McKinsey would never stop making demands on our time, so it was up to us to decide what we were willing to do. It was our responsibility to draw the line.' As the division between work and home gets even more blurred, we need to start drawing our own line.

With a few small tweaks to our mindset, we can begin to be in charge of how and when we consume and generate information, rather than letting it control us.

Chapter 6

All change

What is the most cutting insult the corporate world can bestow? One is suggesting that someone is 'tactical', as opposed to 'strategic'.* However, the most damning insult of all is to imply that your victim is 'resistant to change'. This marks them out as hopelessly old-fashioned and lumbering, unable to keep up with the frenetic pace of whatever probably-not-actually-that-dynamic industry they're working in.

The second part of this section of the book deals with change, and our sense of purpose as employees. I'm initially hesitant to even confront the topic of change in the workplace. What if people mutter behind my back and shun me on LinkedIn? But if we're talking honestly about what makes us dread work, and struggle to focus, then change is often a big part of it.

To placate potential mutterers, I should acknowledge that change in the workplace is often positive. Indeed, it's baked in to the DNA of many of the companies that thrive. You don't want to work for an organization that never questions what it does, or how it does it. Meanwhile, a focus on cost is often what enables a company to turn a profit, which is a fairly fundamental aspect of being in business.**

---

* Someone once casually said that to me at a networking event – I have rarely been more tempted to punch someone.

** Unless they are one of the wave of fashionably unprofitable VC-funded tech firms whose investors are focused purely on growth rather than anything as mundane as profitability.

However, some changes are easier to deal with than others. Investment in a new product line, say, or scaling up headcount to meet rapid growth? These changes are essentially positive. But sometimes corporate change appears ill informed or short sighted. And that's when employees find themselves in for a bumpy ride.

So when does change test employees' motivation?

I'm new here, let's restructure!

Hands up if there's ever been a restructure in your company.

Keep your hand up if that restructure was done by someone reasonably new to the business or department.

Anyone without their hand up, you have my congratulations.

Restructures are often carried out to support new strategies or streamline overweight departments, and they are often instigated by a new or new-ish leader. On the one hand, this is positive – indeed, companies may purposefully hire someone new in order for them to diagnose structural issues within a team, and to make any difficult changes before they get too entrenched. Voila – new structure!

But the new leader is also under pressure to make their mark at the precise point when they don't yet know all the complexities, and this can lead to flawed decisions. One C-level executive in finance tells me: 'So many times, you see the wrong decisions for the wrong reasons. Quite often people make change so that they look good, rather than it being the right thing to do. In my sector, managers move around between departments every few years, so you have limited time to show you've made your mark. The result is endless change for change's sake.'

A programme manager I speak to agrees: 'Oh, senior leadership change a whole division, then three years later move it back. You see so much wasted time and cost because someone new comes in and wants to put their mark on things.'

Spend enough time in the corporate world and the changes become predictable, 'restructuring 101' moves: new leaders mirror the structure of their old company for no particular reason, or they tweak whether the marketing department should report into sales, or whether the product team is part of the technology department. But if redundancies are part of the deal, these leaders may get rid of a crucial role by mistake. People are seen as a cost line on a P&L statement, and not all leaders have full insight into what people actually do. Of course, the mistakes become clear after a while, and people have to switch back – often after the new leader has blithely moved on to pastures new.

Frustratingly, the resulting issues often remain invisible, because it is only at the lower levels that the blow of lost knowledge is felt. Writing in *Forbes*, leadership consultant Jack Zenger states that losing such experts is 'a huge and expensive blow to the organization – but often they fail to show up on anyone's radar screen'.

If nothing else, restructures are just so *disruptive*. As one report from research firm Gartner puts it:

Restructuring disrupts the entire organization. Workflows slow as employees adjust to shifts in reporting, management and goals. Changes disrupt communication and delay decision making.

Dr Judith Mohring, an expert in workplace mental health, tells me, 'endemic uncertainty is built into many workplaces'. She adds, 'Many of these changes in organizations actually achieve very little and raise stress rather than productivity – which in itself is counter-productive'.

Mergers and acquisitions is another high-risk area, and there are lots of them: the United Kingdom alone saw £83.4 billion of M&A activity in 2019. A merger may strengthen geographic coverage or product offering, and executives happily imagine the 'synergies' or 'rationalization' to be achieved by getting rid of duplicate functions. But mergers are often, objectively, a failure. One KPMG report concluded that 83% of mergers failed to deliver shareholder value, with 30% having no impact and 53% of mergers actively destroying shareholder value. However, when asked, 82% of the leaders involved believed shareholder value had been added.

After the excitement of the initial press release fades, it is extremely hard to merge processes, teams and product ranges. In the world of technology, apparently similar product lines can mask entirely different technical architectures, meaning that consolidation efforts are expensive. In March 2021 the share price of the London Stock Exchange (itself a listed company) suffered its biggest daily fall in twenty years because of the higher-than-expected cost of integrating the financial data company Refinitiv: an acquisition that cost £27 billion. Crucially, mergers can consume not only money but also attention, draining focus that could be directed towards innovation. A merger also creates a bigger company, where crucial networks of trust and mutual accountability risk being diluted, increasing the need for process and bureaucracy.

The most complex factors of all, however, include language and culture. The KPMG report mentioned above found that mergers between two companies that share the same language were most likely to succeed, while deals between US and European companies were most likely to face difficulties.

The culture clash created by a merger can be painful. The spirit that has driven the growth of the purchased company may ebb away as its employees wake up to the reality of a bigger firm. David Chancellor, writing for the Chartered Management Institute, puts forward the example of book chain Borders, which was acquired by Kmart back in 1992. He states that the Borders team were 'book people' whereas Kmart was a discount department store chain. Post-acquisition, a lot of the former senior managers from Borders left, as they felt disconnected from Kmart's radically different mission. As Chancellor writes, 'Once it was sold to Kmart, Borders quickly lost the founders' DNA that had made the company so successful.'

Mergers and acquisitions can be a crisis point for the mission and purpose of the acquired company: mission being what the company does and whom it serves; purpose being why it does it. Executive boards know that these things matter. So why are there so many mergers and acquisitions? The trouble is that they just look so alluring, with their promise of scale and cost-cutting. What is more, C-level leaders are under pressure to make big moves quickly. As advisor and business strategist Martin Roll tells me, a touch drily, 'With executive compensation increasingly linked to stock performance, the prospect of more money adds a substantial incentive to pursue a merger than may not be entirely in the best interests of the company.'

And even if every restructure or change in ownership is well thought through, there are just so *many*. Organizational change often feels near-constant; employees are barely out of one when they are plunged into the next. And they know it's only a matter of time until the next leader comes along and changes it all back.

The lure of magic beans

One day I find myself thinking about *Jack and the Beanstalk*. Is it just me, or did Jack take quite a risk with those magic beans? His mother had a single, cherished cow, and Jack swapped it for some magic beans from an old man he met in the street. If I was his mother, I would have been livid. Yet organizations persist in doing something similar, regularly giving up on the agreed plan in order to chase something exciting and new.

I will give an example from my world of software product development. Let's imagine that not long into the year an email comes in from the sales director, copying in everyone he can think of. 'Client X wants a new feature. Jeff says we'll win

£3 million of business if we build it!' If he has a sharp appreciation of human aversion to loss, he may instead write, 'Jeff says
we'll *lose* client X to our most-hated competitor unless we do
this!' Or perhaps Jeff has already blithely sold feature X despite
the minor problem that it does not yet exist.

This is great if Jeff's customer requirement fits in with the
broader strategic direction of the company, or if it identifies a
previously unmet market need. Sometimes, though, the feature
is not even being considered. Indeed, it solves a problem for precisely one client: Jeff's.

The request should be properly prioritized by revenue and
strategic importance but, understandably, no one ever wants
to lose a client, so enormous effort is expended to make it all
happen. The CEO often has a sales or finance background, so
they are on board. Other initiatives that were initially deemed
important for the long-term strategy are temporarily paused,
the change justified by talk of pivoting, quick wins, being nimble,
agile and so on. Multiple teams work hard to deliver the new
feature instead.

Why does this kind of thing happen so often? Well, sales
teams usually push for these tweaks because they are closest
to a company's customers and, frankly, have the hard job of
delivering revenue. I sympathise with this because I have some
(albeit limited) experience of how it feels to be under the inces-
sant pressure of a sales target. One summer, in my late teens,
I sold aerial photographs of peoples' neighbourhoods (yes,
really) door to door in the North Shore suburbs of Chicago.
As a nineteen-year-old South Londoner I knew nothing about
America beyond the eighties teen movies of John Hughes, and
I was amazed to find it was exactly as depicted, right down to
the enormous, plush houses, the fast cars, the sprawling malls
and high schools. (I only realized years later that my sales turf
– Northbrook, Glencoe, Highland Park and other suburbs near
Lake Michigan – happened to be precisely where John Hughes
grew up and filmed his movies.)

My pay was 100% based on commission. No sales, no pay cheque. The pressure to sell, far from home, brought out the worst in some of my colleagues. One person in a rival team was notorious for making questionable assertions to close a sale. Was the $49 frame solid oak? Yes, of course, madam. Your swimming pool is partly obscured by an overhanging tree? No problem, madam, we hold a 'reverse negative' for each print: I'll order you one of those and it will show your pool in all its glory. By the time the print arrived, identical to the original, my morally dubious colleague would be far away back in England.

Let's assume that Jeff's deal finally happens. Perhaps he comes through with the promised £3 million, but more often it turns out there was some hot air and bluster involved, and the deal is actually smaller. The magic beans turn out to be ... well, just beans. No giant beanstalk sprouts outside. Jack and his mother have sold their cow, and now they're just sitting there, feeling hungry.*

The real risk is not that the deal is smaller than was promised: the real concern is the cost of not doing the thing that was originally planned. Often it was something important but, fatally, not urgent. Jock Busuttil, founder of Product People Ltd, rolls his eyes: 'Sometimes an organization needs to invest in a project that won't deliver millions by itself, but plugs a crucial gap in a product range, retains a chunk of customers, or enhances brand perception. These projects would bring in millions in indirect revenue, but they're a long-term play. Sometimes a delay in favour of this year's numbers is just too tempting.'

The concepts of 'minimum viable product' and 'iterative product release' can have an unintended impact. Product teams used to define a product upfront in a detailed document, and then a team of engineers would build it (this is the 'waterfall' methodology). Subsequently, testers would test it, and finally,

---

* It is probably just as well that I don't write picture books for small children.

the company would release the product, crossing its fingers that it still bore some resemblance to market needs.

Now, for many types of product, teams build and release in increments: that is, they start with something basic and evolve it. This is the agile approach, and it has lots of great benefits, such as early feedback and the ability to course-correct if you get new market information. But the whole process is reliant on an *ongoing* set of releases. 'The danger,' says Jock, 'is that a busy executive hears V1 of a product is out, thinks, "box ticked!" and promptly cuts all the funding, leaving the business with a product that still needs a lot more work.' Then, when the product doesn't do everything it was supposed to, *everyone* is impacted – the sales team have to sell something that limps, the marketing team has to get creative when it comes to promoting barely-there features, and the finance department starts asking why it's not making money.

Jock sighs: 'Of course, the board still expect all the features from the product. They ask things like, why is the product's archi-tecture not scalable? And you think, "Er - because you dropped all the funding?"'

If this is the norm, technical teams become accustomed to initiatives getting the chop halfway through the year, and they have to prioritize speed over quality in order to deliver products quickly. Therefore, technical debt (compromises in technology and design) mounts up because things tend to get done quickly instead of properly, all of which slows down future develop-ment. These kinds of manoeuvres lead to a different kind of Sunday night dread: that your company is making short-term decisions that will one day come back to bite them.

Companies that constantly chase magic beans are not going to lead the way when it comes to the next big revenue-gener-ating product. Dropping strategic project X means that, a year later, they find they don't have anything sustainable to sell, so they have to do it again. It's a vicious circle.

Cost-cutting

Going back to *Jack and the Beanstalk*, why on earth does Jack's mother get him to take the cow to the market in the first place? It's infuriating. Rather than exchanging it for food, which is a very short-term gain, surely she should should keep the cow for an ongoing supply of milk? Jack's mother, I conclude, must be a senior executive who is under pressure to achieve some short-term cost-cutting.

Efficiency is a noble and, indeed, essential aim, and if teams are bloated or processes are ridiculous, then it is an executive board's job to streamline them. Occasionally, however, it can feel as though cost-cutting is done by someone who isn't close enough to the detail.

To the employee who finds themself in the middle of a cost-cutting exercise, it can feel frustrating and counterproductive. One operations manager tells me: 'We got rid of an operational team in a hurry because no one wanted to fund them. They'd been told their job was no longer valued and was not being replaced, so they left without documenting how anything worked. There was a small, short-term cost saving on salaries. Then stuff started breaking. Now I'm paying way more for consultants to work it all out.'

That said, short-termism is no fun for those at the top either. In his 2020 book *Winning Now, Winning Later*, former CEO David Cote describes joining industrial conglomerate Honeywell in 2002 only to inherit a 'train wreck' of a firm with an entrenched 'make the quarter' mindset. Cote makes it clear that there was nothing illegal going on – everything fell within permitted accounting practice – but 'the entire organisation was gaming the system to try to make their numbers each quarter'. Cote writes:

> None of these actions strengthened the company by either increasing sales or reducing costs. Rather, the actions were

one-time transactions designed to make Honeywell more profitable on paper.

The vicious circle produced by cutting costs too heavily to meet short-term targets – whether in administration, marketing, headcount or R&D – is more likely to put a company at risk than to help it thrive. Employees who believe the purpose of the company was to deliver a great product, or help people solve a problem, feel disenchanted when it all turns out to just be about revenue or profit. Yet, a cost-based decision, however dubious, has one simplistic advantage: it is numerically quantifiable and therefore easy to defend. The hidden costs, in terms of lost engagement and motivation, are much harder to enumerate. As such they – and their long-term impact – tend to remain hidden.

Dude, where's my why?

Of course, some organizational change is necessary and inevitable. After all, companies that don't balance the books are not going to be around for long.

However, there can be a communication gap. The higher echelons are coached in the art and necessity of the swift restructure or strategic review, as a quick glance at any business website or leadership book will tell you. The vast majority of an organization's employees are not. They focus on doing the jobs they were hired to do, and the primacy of the cost-cutting axe leaves them puzzled and nursing unexpected wounds.

Sometimes simply diagnosing the required change causes friction: when an external consultant or strategy expert is brought in to assess what needs doing, for example. A consultant is usually brought in by one of the executive board when they need something to be assessed or sorted out, and it is precisely their third-party status that will give them an insightful, independent viewpoint. But the rationality of an external recommendation doesn't mean that permanent employees won't rail against the experience. Why are an interloper's views being valued over their own? Do senior managers not care about all their effort and hard work? One employee nods: 'We had two external consultants brought in recently but the reasons why were very opaque, so it sowed a lot of mistrust. It turned out they were there to report back on who was expendable. I get it, that's how business goes, but it felt so insulting.'

Scott Keller and Colin Price, the authors of *Beyond Performance: How Great Organizations Build Ultimate Competitive Advantage*, found that no less than 39% of failed change efforts had 'employee resistance to change' as a factor.

Sometimes, resistance is due to a lack of information from above about why something is happening. This can happen for a number of reasons. Companies may feel that it would undermine the middle tiers of management if the upper echelons were to communicate directly with everyone. Instead, they favour a manager 'cascade' to transmit information down through the ranks. But this presents a real challenge for everyone involved, because it is supremely difficult to transmit important messages through numerous layers of management. There are three distinct challenges: the opportunity for two-way questioning is lost, something is always omitted in translation, and the communication burden is placed on the most overloaded people in a business.

One marketing manager tells me how badly a corporate merger was communicated at his workplace: 'The chief executive sent out a long email about the sale of the business to his direct reports. It had probably been proofread and PR-approved a dozen times, but everyone I spoke to had a different interpretation of what it said. One told me, "We're going to be rich!" whereas another said, "We're all out of a job!" More importantly, the CEO's direct reports were supposed to transmit the message downwards to all their teams, but many did not realize this. The chief executive was confident everyone had been briefed, but this was far from the case.'

A head of analytics for a software firm recalls a strategic shift to building products in the cloud rather than hosted 'on-premise'. This involved making several legacy experts redundant and creating new roles elsewhere. But during the transition period many teams still relied on the old experts, and there were a number of operational challenges. He says: 'The technical director briefed his immediate team, of course. He focused deeply on those who were impacted. But they were demoralized and not the right people to spread the word. He thought the other stakeholders would hear the news in the right way, but the message was jumbled up with the employees' negative emotions about losing their jobs. It was a classic case of thinking the job was done, when it was not.'

Occasionally, leaders are indeed reticent to explain why something is happening. It feels supremely uncomfortable, or they feel it undermines their authority by inviting those further down the hierarchy to question their decision making. Mostly, though, leaders appreciate how crucial it is to communicate well. They simply underestimate how many times they need to repeat a message, or they fail to appreciate how different things can look from a different level. The CEO isn't callously cutting the call centre you've spent five years building up: to them it is just a cost line in the P&L. Meanwhile, you're not trying to scupper their plan to increase operating leverage: you just want to run a good call centre. And what on earth is operating leverage, anyway?

Everyone would tell you they communicate well. Everyone knows it is crucial. But it is surprisingly hard to get right.

The price of blurred vision

What does this constant to-ing and fro-ing do to an organization? Well, very little, on the surface. No one admits openly that they find the constant flux a little wearing. Everyone knows they need to be professional. Yet being buffeted by other people's cost-driven projects impacts both your sense of purpose and any feeling of autonomy or control, which is, unsurprisingly, not a great place to find yourself.

On the occasions where there is overt and sustained pressure to prioritize revenue – a feeling that this is 'the' motivational force for a company – the results can be catastrophic. When Boeing merged with McDonnell Douglas in 1997, Harry Stonecipher became Boeing's new president and chief operating officer. He told the *Chicago Tribune* in 2004:

> When people say I changed the culture of Boeing, that was the intent, so it's run like a business rather than a great engineering firm. It is a great engineering firm, but people invest in a company because they want to make money.

The 2020 US government report into the two Boeing 737 MAX aircraft crashes says of Stonecipher's words, 'Those sentiments, according to many observers and current and former Boeing employees, infected the company.' The report cites one of the many attempts by senior plant supervisor Ed Pierson to halt the 737 MAX production line to resolve safety issues:

> According to Mr. Pierson's testimony to the Committee in December 2019, when he walked into Mr. Campbell's office, Mr. Campbell asked him: 'Why are you here?' ... Pierson recalled telling Mr. Campbell: 'In ... military operations, if we have these kinds of indications of unstable safety type of things, we would stop.' ... Mr. Campbell responded: 'The military is not a profit-making organization.'

Ed Pierson retired in frustration in August 2018, less than three months before a Boeing 737 MAX crashed off Indonesia, killing 189 people. Months later a second aircraft crashed in Ethiopia, killing 157 passengers and crew.

The report noted that many Boeing employees 'understand they once worked for a great engineering firm, and many hope that they will again in the future'. After the publication of the report, Boeing issued a statement:

> We have learned many hard lessons as a company from the accidents of Lion Air Flight 610 and Ethiopian Airlines Flight 302, and from the mistakes we have made. As this report recognizes, we have made fundamental changes to our company as a result, and continue to look for ways to improve. Change is always hard and requires daily commitment, but we as a company are dedicated to doing the work.

Not all companies shoulder such heavy consequences. Neither do companies overtly declare that they exist to drive revenue. Companies don't put 'We want to make lots of money' in their mission statements. They write customer-facing things like 'We want to deliver the best product for our customers' or 'We strive to solve problem X.' Yet organizations still jump on profit-centred activity that undermines their aspirations. I hear of a TV channel whose sale to a big media company had a sweetener built in: a bonus for each show that reached more than 500,000 viewers in the period before the sale closed. Rather than seeing it as a nice potential perk, this bonus was baked in to the financial forecasts surrounding the sale. As a result, the commissioning team had to drop everything in pursuit of ratings. Given the long lead time on programming, this obliged them to think of shows that both would rate highly and could be made very quickly. The results? Among others, a hastily produced show about nudists and a seance with a dead mega-celebrity that was voted by a popular poll as the worst show of the year. The channel's avowed mission until that point in its history? Top-quality programming.

Chapter 7

More than money

Can the temptation to grasp short-term profit be changed? When it comes to companies and their purpose, there's an elephant in the room: sometimes organizations are not as free as they appear to be. Short-term decision making is baked in to many publicly listed companies due to the pressure they are under to meet earnings guidance or demonstrate profits. This situation is reinforced by the near-term, twelve-month cycle of the financial year and its accompanying annual bonus. It's been that way since at least the 1970s, when shareholder value was held aloft as the key driving force of business, propelled by thinking from right-leaning economists such as Milton Friedman, who stated in a 1970 *New York Times* article that 'the social responsibility of business is to increase its profits'.

The issue may be the desire to demonstrate consistent profit growth. Former Honeywell CEO David Cote writes:

> Every quarter we felt pressure to find additional, potentially destructive, solutions not just to make comparable numbers but higher ones, because we needed to show increasing profits.

Or the issue may be one not of profit levels per se, but of being consistent with market expectations. As the non-executive director of a FTSE 100 company tells me over Zoom, 'Miss the numbers by 10% and you're into profit warning territory. It's just how it works. You could have stellar growth but if you've promised the market more, you're in danger of being lambasted.'

In one FCLT Global survey, 88% of executives agreed that a long-term horizon was best for financial performance, but 65% of respondents reported increased pressure for short-term results over the previous five-year period. Meanwhile, time horizons are becoming ever more condensed: 87% of executives reported pressure to deliver within a two-year horizon, compared with 79% three years previously.

This is not helped by the decreasing average length of tenure for an executive board member. A few decades ago a member of the board might have risen up through their company and settled near the top until they received their golden carriage clock at their retirement party. In 2019 PricewaterhouseCoopers reported that the median tenure of a CEO was just five years. These CEOs are only given a short time to prove themselves, and they are likely to be judged on the financial results they preside over during their tenure, not the groundwork they lay for their successors.

I come across one report by management consultancy McKinsey that assesses what makes a CEO exceptional. The report defines as 'exceptional' the CEOs that increased returns to their companies' shareholders by more than 500% during their tenure.* But is this level of return the best measure of success? Is it viable over the long term?

I speak with Tom Caddick, a former chief investment officer for an international bank. He tells me: 'The pressure to deliver shareholder value is very difficult to change.' Can shareholders be persuaded to take a longer-term view? Maybe via great investor-relations teams, who sell the long-term vision? Tom is doubtful: 'I don't think there is any such thing as an understanding

---

* Perhaps unsurprisingly given the definition of success, the outstanding CEOs were 19% more likely than the average CEO to undertake a cost-reduction programme during their spell in charge.

public investor base. People buy shares and risk their capital for the expectation of a return. That's just how it works.'

It's complicated. Many of the biggest buyers of shares are pension funds and they need to generate a return to fund the retirement of people like you and me. We can't have our cake and eat it.

'Stay private!' exclaims one CEO that I interview. 'That way, you don't have to waste energy on short-termism. If lucky, you can be selective about your investors and find private funds prepared for long-term returns.'

This view is supported by 2013 research from MIT Economics, who found that publicly traded US businesses scored less well on measures of integrity than similar private companies. The researchers theorized that the pressure of shareholder return led to decisions that compromised integrity.

Where does this economic reality leave our sense of purpose? Do we accept that corporate purpose, mission statements and so on, only go so far?

From shareholders to stakeholders

In 1888, in Merseyside, England, William Lever started building Port Sunlight, a village destined for the workers in his thriving soap manufacture business. Its construction was driven by an ethos that Lever termed 'shared prosperity'. All the homes had running water and some bore architectural flourishes such as leaded windows and exposed timbers – unheard-of in the functional worker accommodation elsewhere in the United Kingdom.

Encouraged to spend their leisure time on self-improvement, employees enjoyed use of a library, a gym, a concert hall, a theatre and a public swimming pool. William Lever's soap manufacturing company went from strength to strength, eventually becoming the multinational consumer goods company Unilever.

Fast forward more than 120 years. In 2009 Unilever's then-CEO, Paul Polman, was brand new to the job. Deciding that the company needed to reconnect with its core values, he took his management team to Port Sunlight, the workers' village so emblematic of its founder's vision of responsible capitalism. Polman and his team decided to make their business model more responsible and pledged to massively reduce the company's environmental impact.

In one of his first speeches from Unilever HQ in London, Polman proceeded to greatly startle commentators. To kick things off, Polman told the markets that he wasn't going to report quarterly results any more: Unilever's view would be long-term. Polman then announced:

> If you buy into this long-term value-creation model, which is equitable, which is shared, which is sustainable, then come and invest with us. If you don't buy into this, I respect you as a human being, but don't put your money in our company.

The *Financial Times* journalist Michael Skapinker was in the audience at the time, and recalls his astonishment in a 2018 article: 'I was startled by it. I had never before heard a business boss tell a substantial proportion of his shareholders to get lost.'

In an interview five years later with Margareta Barchan of Business School Lausanne, Polman explained:

> A lot of companies are driven by the short-termism of the markets. [They] make short-term decisions that often go against the long-term viability of the company. ... It's very easy to show more profits, if that's what you want, by cutting investments in training and development of your people or your IT systems. And you can do that for a few years but in the long term, you erode your company.

However, by this time a subtle shift had taken place: Polman was no longer seen as an outlier, but as a trailblazer. Business Roundtable, an association of major business leaders, had espoused shareholder primacy since 2007, but in 2019 they issued a new 'Statement on the purpose of a corporation'. It stated that leaders should steer their companies 'for the benefit of all stakeholders – customers, employees, suppliers, communities and shareholders'. In 2019 the pledge was adopted by 181 American CEOs.

In July 2020, a few months before becoming the Democratic presidential nominee, Joe Biden declared in a speech:

> It's way past time we put an end to the era of shareholder capitalism, the idea the only responsibility a corporation has is with shareholders. That's simply not true. It's an absolute farce. They have a responsibility to their workers, their community, to their country.

So, not only can companies choose to redefine their relationship with shareholders, but they are supported by a broader change in sentiment. Move over shareholders: stakeholder value is the new buzzword.

This is compounded by a demographic shift: a sense that the 'old guard' is on the way out. New generations of workers, fed up with corporate scandals and an exhausted planet, are calling time on short-termism. A 2017 Kantar Futures/American Express report found that, globally, 75% of millennials expect their workplaces to deliver both profit and a genuine purpose. This brings hope for longer-term decision making and sustainable return.

Of course, words are one thing: action is another. The Business Roundtable pledge has its critics, who point out that it still needs to translate into real-world change. However, these high-level shifts mean that, if CEOs and boards declare long-term goals, they are likely to find an increasingly receptive audience.

By the time David Cote left Honeywell in 2017, after fifteen years at the helm, the company's market capitalization had increased from $20 billion to nearly $100 billion. Cote achieved this in part by emphasizing the long-term nature of the business both to staff and to the markets. Cote insisted on intellectual rig-our from his team in setting long-term goals and making them realistic. As he said: 'This isn't easy or glamourous work, but it must be done if you want your business to perform well years into the future.'

Indeed, going beyond the short-term consistently pays off. One McKinsey/FCLT Global study found that firms with a long-term view outperformed their more short-term rivals on every measure they tracked, from revenue growth (47% higher) to economic profit (81% higher).

Meanwhile, the faith of long-term investors in Unilever was rewarded, with Paul Polman presiding over a total shareholder return of 290% during his tenure. Over that same period the business improved the livelihoods of more than 700,000 small-holder farmers and 1.6 million small-scale retailers, cut its waste impact by 29% and sourced 56% of its agricultural raw materials sustainably.

So, despite shareholder pressure, companies *can* choose to make longer-term decisions rather than racing into yet another cost-cutting exercise, or chasing their tail in search of near-term revenue. But what if you are not a visionary CEO? What if you are somewhere in the middle of your organization?

The grassroots mission

By 2012, the denim factory in the sleepy Welsh town of Cardi-gan was long gone – another victim of globalization. But the entrepreneur David Hieatt noticed something: all over town, the expertise once needed by the factory remained. In the coffee shops, the pub – even in the driving schools – the employees got on with their jobs, but they also knew how to make jeans. Concealed just under the town's surface, with no outlet, was a rich vein of craftsmanship and knowledge.

Hieatt decided to found a high-end jeans company, Hiut Denim, which now makes 150 pairs of jeans a week. The company supplies worldwide, including to celebrities, and it has a crystal clear principle: do one thing well. That thing is to make jeans. If retailers ask them to branch out into sweatshirts or bobble hats, they refuse. They even refuse to make more pairs of jeans per year, because they're not about quantity. 'We are clear in our mind,' David Hieatt told Mark Robinson of design website OEN, 'we are here to make the best jeans we can, not the most jeans we can.'

A strong sense of purpose is not unique to high-end clothing brands. The small London-based company Envirobuild Materials, which supplies eco-friendly garden and construction materials, donates 10% of its profits to the Rainforest Trust, and they buy all their office furniture and equipment second hand. More than half of their team cycle to work.* These are great tales of putting purpose before profit.

Obviously, companies such as Hiut Denim are privately owned, and as such they are free to define their own relationship with profit. While researching these kinds of company I also notice how often they feature dashing, maverick CEOs with tousled locks. But what if you are just an employee, and your CEO is more the humourless, tense-jawed type, whose primary passion is maximizing his next bonus? After all, not all companies are ripe for reinvention. Some are too big, too entrenched in their ways – or maybe they simply don't care enough. How do you, as an individual, motivate yourself? What do you aim for?

I'm struck by something that David Hieatt says. He explains that he had the idea for his jeans company more than a year before he acted on it. He knew it was a sound idea, but he dismissed it and literally put the plan on a shelf. Then one day, while out running, his former designer called him to say he had loved the denim idea. He told David he should make the jeans in Cardigan, his former home town. David says: 'Something just struck

---

* I'm also happy to note that they refuse to stock artificial turf because of its negative environmental impact.

me as he said it. I had worked out my "why". This jeans company was about getting a town that used to make jeans, to make them again. ... It was all about the town.'

You need to find your why.

The trouble is, as individuals we often have a complicated relationship with 'why' – the reason why we get up on Monday morning to do our jobs. Many people describe a creeping sense that they are wasting their lives in their current role. This hits them on Sunday because, after two days of freedom, they have to go back to something their heart is not really into. If this is the case, then it is certainly best to start looking for something new.

However, people in perfectly interesting jobs are also often sold the myth of having to be utterly in love, beyond any doubt, with what they do – just take a cursory scroll through any life coach's Instagram feed. 'Find a job you love, and you'll never work a day in your life!' trill the motivational slogans. So we worry that we don't constantly love our work, which is a tough ask when our poor, beleaguered jobs also usually need to serve a solid financial purpose. (Also, lovely creative jobs have a downside: as soon as you shackle them to the obligation of earning you a living, you might stop loving the thing you love.) Generally, it is important not to beat yourself up if you do something reasonable with your working week that brings in the financial stability you need, and you choose to follow your passion for extreme sports or crochet in your spare time. *That's OK, too.*

So your personal, private 'why' may simply be a reasonable amount of money in return for a reasonably engaging role (perhaps don't put this on LinkedIn). Ideally, you also need a professional 'why' – a decent organizational purpose.

If, however, organizational purpose seems lacking, and you feel like a cog in a giant machine, then you and your team may need to find your own 'why'. It might be something really small and simple. Ask yourself who your department helps. How can you help them further? Or, if you're stuck for inspiration, look back at the early days of the business. Were the founders guided by a particular principle, or by a problem they wanted to solve?

Purists will observe that everyone in an organization must be led by the same purpose or it will lead to trouble. And they are quite right: you want your 'why' to complement the overarching aim of the organization, not to conflict with it. But centring your small team around something that drives you, however small, has real power.*

The same purists will also point out that at some point, the overall pressures of the organization will burst in and pop the small team's positive bubble. This is also true, but what's the worst-case scenario? That you improve engagement and morale most of the time? Well that's not a bad outcome. It's better than feeling rudderless, or like you are only there to drive profits.

Even in big, listed companies, if you can work out what you and your team stand for, then many subsequent decisions fall into place, guided by that one principle. If you find yourself in a company where change is the norm, it will act as an anchoring and motivating force. Let the broader company race after magic beans. You and your team have decided that you want to solve as many customer problems as you can or provide the best ever user experience – or whatever else it is you want to achieve. How you pursue your purpose may change, other factors may temporarily derail you, but it remains your guiding star.

And purpose brings results. Scott Keller and Mary Meaney, authors of *Leading Organizations: Ten Timeless Truths*, found that teams working towards a shared mission are nearly twice as likely to deliver above-median financial performance.

Of course, it's not always easy to find your purpose. What if you are faced with particularly tough or unlikely circumstances?

---

* Plus, there are worse things for a team than a minor note of rebellion: it will make you feel like you're all in something together.

111

The power of storytelling

One morning in 2011, brand consultant Claire Lowson found herself in the lift at a big UK bank, surrounded by unsmiling faces. With the 2008 financial crash still fresh in peoples' minds, the atmosphere in some departments remained subdued. By now, millions of column inches and countless hours of TV coverage had examined the role of the banking sector in precipitating a global crisis. The business unit that Claire had been brought in to work with was generally considered the hardest to work in. Tasked with disposing of non-core assets as part of a UK government bailout, the people assigned to work in this unit felt doubly hard done by. First, it was tough work. And second, there was a deadline to wrap up the unit: effectively they were working themselves out of a job. On paper, it wasn't a great recipe for team morale.

Suddenly, a woman in the lift caught sight of Claire's visitor pass. Her face lit up: 'Oh, you're the people working with non-core assets! It looks so fantastic in there. It feels so completely different to the rest of the business. I wish I worked there.'

Claire tells me: 'That's when I knew our efforts were working.'

Her team was tasked with shaping the non-core team's identity and purpose. Claire explains: 'It wasn't quick, but it built upon itself over time.'

'What did you do, exactly?' I ask.

'We got the team telling their story, because storytelling gets you thinking about what you're doing and why. We asked, why were they there? And something started cropping up. People described that they were doing totally unique problem solving – no one had been tasked with anything like this before.'

The unprecedented nature of the work had initially been a massive negative in people's minds, but it quickly became the centre of a much more positive story. As Claire says: 'We found so many positives. Because the work was complex and unique, it demanded constant innovation. The team started getting more and more confident in putting their heads above the parapet. Consequently, they pushed their skill set and experience far beyond that of their peers in other units.' The team had found their 'why'.

It also became clear to the team that their work was far from being a dead end. 'The team themselves soon realised that they would be eminently employable afterwards,' Claire tells me.

To help embed a distinct identity, the unit was encouraged to have a personality and character very different from the rest of the business. As Claire recounts: 'We used a different colour for the brand of the business unit. It was a fight initially, as you can imagine, but it was essential to establish the significance of the task in hand and to give the unit a special status. We used straightforward language and put up signs to make new people – there were lots coming in – feel quickly at home and part of the team. We talked to everyone in a human way, not a business way. It was simple really, but you know what? People went from feeling despondent to feeling strong. They changed their story.'

Claire pauses: 'It just goes to show that with a human focus, you can take a small part of a company and change how people feel about their work – even in the most challenging of contexts.'

Of course, having your own clear sense of purpose doesn't stop change coming your way. An organization will invariably change course – and frequently – in response to new information or market conditions. But even when change is positive, too much of it risks grinding people down. Are there ways to make it less painful for everyone?

The shift to 'why'

I'm standing on a chair clutching a microphone. It's not a comfortable position to be in, in any sense, but it's the only way to be heard over the babble of 200 software engineers, data scientists and others in the massive conference room.

My colleagues and I are halfway through a 'PI Planning' session. This stands for Programme Increment planning, and in our case it is a big, two-day event where we plan what features we will build in our software over the upcoming twelve weeks. As the VP of the product team, my role is to steer what everyone will build and why. (My audience are the clever ones working on the tricky bits, like 'how'.) I speak into the microphone.

'Hi everyone – can I have your attention. I'm sorry to interrupt your work, but we need to change what one team is doing.' I remind the group that across all six teams, one feature above all others has to be delivered for customers – but the team in charge of that feature have just told me they won't get it all finished during the twelve-week period. They'll need help. Team Three therefore needs to pause their work and pitch in. 'I'll come and talk to Team Three now,' I say.

Climbing down off my chair and heading over to see the team that has just spent a day preparing a different feature, my heart sinks. I want to smile but they all look so disgruntled that I find myself wincing instead. 'I'm sorry,' I say. 'How are you feeling?' One person at the rear of the cluster shrugs. Another, closer in, says: 'I guess I feel like we've just wasted our day.' I tell them that we definitely need to pick up today's prep work again in the next PI Planning session, but explain the crucial customer need that is met by the priority feature. I talk about the alternatives: 'We thought about stopping Team Four, but you have the best skill set to pick up this particular work. So this feels like the best compromise. What do you think?'

I'm not enjoying myself. Until we started having these events, this kind of change would have been passed to the engineers via someone else in my team, and I wouldn't have had to see Team Three's forlorn faces. But after a few moments I feel the atmosphere thawing. Someone smiles and says, 'Don't worry, Helen – we'll get started right away.'

The credit is partly due to this group being full of particularly friendly and professional people, but it is also due to the events themselves, which are a massive investment in engagement and transparency. A PI Planning event – part of the Scaled Agile Framework – puts everyone involved in creating a product in a room together for two days: leaders and team members alike, all working through every planned feature. It's intense. Complexity is discovered as we go, and trade-offs have to be made, but we're all in it together. It's also physical, as you spend most of the day on your feet. But your sense of tiredness at the end of the day feels well earned.

I don't really like the Scaled Agile Framework. It feels like a heavyweight process, and too much process makes me irritable, because I want to get on with making things. But I love PI Planning events because of the palpable sense of teamwork, and the way they make communication super-productive. If a decision needs to be made, we can swiftly pull together the right group to discuss it. It resembles what social philosopher Charles Handy describes as a 'task culture', where the project goal is all important and 'expert power' is given more weight than status. This is ideal for the world of software development, where speed of reaction to the market is crucial. And at the same time, these events don't just tolerate change, they bake it in. They make sure that everyone knows what is happening and, crucially, why it is happening.

One of the most powerful ways to ease the pain of a 'sudden swerve' may also be one of the most simple: leaders forcing themselves both to face those impacted and to explain 'why' more often. The transparency takes the sting out of it. This may sound incredibly minor, but sometimes it's the minor things that count. In psychologist Ellen Langer's classic 1978 research study conducted in a university library, researchers determined that 50% of people queuing for a Xerox machine responded positively to a request to jump the queue when the word 'because' was included in the sentence. It worked even when the explanation did not bear scrutiny, such as 'because I have to make copies'. Simply adding the word 'because' made the message *fifty* percent more effective. The researchers theorized that hearing the word 'because' is a kind of shortcut: that the human brain likes to perceive a reason for a request, and hearing keywords that correspond to a reason makes them likely to help.

'We already do that!' protest those tasked with communicating the latest change to the rest of their company. It is possible, however, that they've communicated the message several times, knowing that repetition is key to success, but focused only on the 'what'. Maybe the team held five webinars, during which they told everyone five times about the torturous new way of submitting expenses. But did they talk about the thought process behind the decision making, or about the alternatives they could have chosen, or about why they settled on that approach?

For those in charge of communicating about change, it also works best if you are honest about how change feels. I speak to workplace mental health expert Dr Judith Mohring and describe to her how, in my world of software development, being relaxed about change is an unwritten rule of professional life: embrace it or be seen as hopelessly behind the times. But deep down, change can be unsettling. Do we all just need to toughen up?

Mohring is emphatic: 'Firstly, change involves uncertainty and loss of control – so of course it's stressful. Also, it's really emotionally invalidating for change to always be presented as a positive. Leaders need to acknowledge that change is difficult. You have to speak to people's reality.'

The most powerful tool is even simpler: involvement. Involve those who will be affected in the decision itself. This is why bringing in an external consultant to diagnose a problem, while rational, often creates friction: those expected to actually carry out their recommendations may feel excluded and undervalued. Dr Stephen Covey, the author of *The Seven Habits of Highly Effective People*, famously said: 'Without involvement, there is no commitment.'

In the informal, collaborative huddles of PI Planning, the decision-making group is based not on rank but on involvement in the issue at stake. Everyone is involved and everyone can chip in, so there tends to be high acceptance of the final decision. If it affects the wider group, we will then update everyone.

In the broader workplace, leaders may not feel able to engage employees so often. Perhaps the situation is particularly complex or thorny, so they feel it is best to make decisions in a small group. Or maybe a group discussion might require a leader to show indecision – something they don't want their team to see. Perhaps they think that people don't want to hear uncertainty around bad news, believing that it's better to provide something certain.

However, if anything, involvement works better for bad news than for good. People are better than you would think at taking bad news, *so long as they feel involved in the decision-making process.* For example, I have just received an email from my local borough council in London asking me for ideas to avoid the closure of my local library. I know they'll knock it down and build yet another horrible block of flats, but I like feeling that I've been consulted.

What the library consultation people have picked up on is simple: never underestimate the extent to which people want their voices to be heard. In a *Harvard Business Review* article, Joel Brockner, a professor of business at Columbia Business School, describes working with a financial institution whose operational managers were resisting a restructure. It turned out that the managers felt senior leadership did not appreciate the scale of the change being requested. Notably, when they were finally listened to, the managers didn't even ask for extra resources. Brockner tells us that 'they simply wanted those at the top to recognize their difficult plight'.

Working alongside Rutgers Business School professor Phyllis Siegel, Brockner found that providing good reasons for decisions and treating people with respect were more important for reducing workplace stress levels than expensive perks designed to help employees manage their work–life balance. Stress isn't necessarily about the number of hours worked but the emotional climate of those hours, and how involved you feel in what is happening to you.

When it comes to finalizing the plan at PI Planning, everyone is involved. I always warn my husband that he has to pick up the kids on a PI Planning day, because every single person in the room has a confidence vote. If approval doesn't rise above a certain level, no one leaves: any issues are addressed until everyone has faith in the plan. It is time intensive and expensive, and everyone consumes their body weight in cake, but PI Planning always give me that warm, fuzzy feeling that comes from a strong team pursuing a shared goal.

And do you know what? The decisions that get made don't even need to be perfect. Decisions are rarely perfect. But people can generally accept that something has to change so long as they know what was going through their leaders' heads, they understand the alternatives that those leaders preferred to avoid, and they know why they landed where they did. What people don't like, funnily enough, is just being told to get on with it.

Focus: ideas

The following ideas are split into two sections: those relating to data overload and those relating to change and purpose.

Ideas for the top

Data overload

♦ For headspace and creativity, consider following the lead of manufacturing firm 3M, where for more than seventy years staff have been able to spend 15% of their time pursing innovative ideas that excite them. The Post-it note, which 3M produces 50 billion of per year, was born out of this creative time. However, even 3M has to guard this time against profit pressure, so don't initiate a 15% rule unless you can stick to it (no pun intended).*

♦ Stop talking about work–life integration. People deserve to switch off. Don't shackle everyone to a 24/7 culture via the Trojan horse of flexibility.

♦ Dissuade escalation of issues: ensure escalators have picked up the phone first, or tried to talk face to face with the person from whom they need something.

---

* Google does something similar with its famous 20% time, but this example did not offer a Post-it related pun.

♦ Banning meetings on certain days is well intentioned but can push them into other days that then become back-to-back meeting territory. Ask people what they think would work best.

♦ Consider using network analysis to identify your most networked and valuable people. One McKinsey study found that only 10% of the fifty most value-creating roles in a company report directly to the CEO, with 60% being two levels down and 20% further down still. Once you identify these people, ask what you can do to help them with their workload.

♦ Identify and help those who are knowledge bottlenecks – the experts who get brought into every email thread and every decision. People will always prefer the expert to attend a meeting, but they can't do everything. Get them to train a few colleagues in their area of expertise, to help spread the load. If that doesn't work, be supportive when they occasionally drop a ball.

♦ Admin help for mid-tier employees pays for itself. Consider the cost saving in booking just a handful of air fares early instead of last minute. If giving admin help to individuals below C-level is a political hot potato, look at the business case for team assistant positions. Everyone benefits that way, and the assistant is often a great candidate for internal promotion as they get to know the ropes incredibly well.

♦ If they are office based, leaders should sit with their team rather than with their peers. This is the best way to understand daily workload and pressure. Nothing says 'I don't care' more than a leader sitting on a different floor.

♦ Make performance objectives editable as needed. If objectives are too rigid, the year-end review may ignore the fact that someone was asked to prioritize five different things for most of the year.

♦ Consider whether apparent efficiencies – either through automation or centralization – are definitely all they are cracked up to be. Before changing a system to self-service, consider the cost of having specialist staff manage all their own recruitment administration, purchase orders and IT hardware/software requests. Is there a middle ground?

♦ Unless something has genuinely been automated, avoid the temptation to sell people the idea of 'self-service' as a wonderful opportunity: just be upfront about it saving money.

♦ If in charge of internal system change, make sure success criteria include positive user experience as well as cost-related metrics.

♦ There's usually something that is making the flood of messages and meetings worse than it needs to be. Is a fear of blame making people too consensus-led, thereby increasing the volume of emails? Are too many initiatives being launched at once? Does some dreadful system ask you to approve every single request your team makes to the IT department? A quick high-level analysis can yield interesting answers.

Change and purpose

♦ Make decisions as close as possible to where the information is, rather than by hierarchy. You'll get more direct input from those that know, and better buy-in.

♦ Consider helping leaders with feelings of discomfort about delivering bad news. If everyone can acknowledge that discomfort is a normal reaction, it can make it easier to have difficult conversations when necessary.

♦ Where applicable, include long-term incentives in executive compensation.

♦ 'Magic beans' requests from the sales team should be signed off not only by the head of the commercial team but also by the chief technology officer or similar. The product team need to carry out an objective assessment of whether the unmet user requirement is real, pervasive, urgent and valuable. For example, is the client who is asking for a new feature really going to leave if they don't get it? Could their problem be solved another way?

♦ A merger is not just about hard metrics: organizational culture is the invisible glue. One KPMG study found that mergers were 26% more likely than average to be successful if they focused on resolving cultural issues early in the discussions rather than leaving them until the post-deal period.

♦ Do not invest in a new product without being prepared to fund it for its lifetime, including ongoing feature development and maintenance. Underfunding a commercially necessary product is the equivalent of setting up your sales force – and your loyal, early-adopting customers – to fail.

♦ To help make the right decisions when costs do need to be cut, practice management by walking around. Former QAS Ltd CEO Simon Worth says: 'You need to be hungry for knowledge: you need to know the business and you need to know the people themselves. One year, when QAS Ltd was expanding fast, I spent six months on the road, travelling to all our offices and spending time with employees while they did their jobs. There are no short cuts.' (Note: while most members of the executive board intend to spend more time 'on the shop floor', most severely lack the time to be the leader they wish to be. For every hour in a 'town hall', where a CEO is wheeled out to talk for an hour, try to also spend an hour with employees at their desks.)

♦ Ever-increasing role specialization means that individuals find it hard to see the results of their efforts. Help people see the impact of their work by sharing stories of satisfied customers and what precisely they like about your company's service or product. This happens routinely within customer-facing departments, but extend it out to the teams that are not customer facing, too.

♦ Most companies need a strategic plan that includes long-term goals. This is not the same thing as asking for ideas at budget time and prioritizing them by revenue. Don't forget the crucial section on what you're *not* doing. As David Hieatt of Hiut Denim says: 'The great companies are defined by the things that they say no to.'

Ideas for you

Data overload

♦ If you are consistently overloaded with new tasks, the classic advice is to ask your manager to identify which of your existing tasks you can drop. By all means try this, but in practice they will still want all the existing tasks to be done as well.* Try asking your manager where on the cost–time–quality triangle each task sits. Draw the triangle if need be. For example, does your manager need something quickly and cheaply, meaning they accept it might be of only average quality? Or do they want something high quality but don't have any budget for it, in which case it will take a longer time? This is a simple way to identify the wiggle room for each task.

---

* Annoying, isn't it?

♦ Create simple changes of scene. Sit outside for a call. Move seats, or swivel your laptop and chair to face a different bit of the room. If you are office based, have meetings in a nearby cafe, or 'talk while you walk' at lunchtime.*

♦ Ask your boss to colour-code or otherwise flag emails that come with a short deadline so they don't get accidentally overlooked.

♦ If you find yourself replying to an irritating email in the heat of the moment, try saving it to send the next morning. Keep your message in your drafts folder overnight and then review it first thing the next day. You will often find yourself able to reply with more perspective.

♦ Remember to congratulate yourself on what you *have* accomplished during the day rather than beating yourself up for what remains on your to-do list. There will always be something left to do: that's why you're employed on an ongoing basis and not just for one day.

Change and purpose

♦ Insist on knowing why. As management coach Clive Smith says: 'It is your right to demand clarity. You're allowed to ask for the rationale behind decisions. If done consistently, those at the top will have to start providing more insight as standard.'

♦ If you're in a leadership role and your organization relies on a downwards cascade of information, make sure you are actually passing on the information, so that those under you are not missing out. When you are busy, it's easy to assume everyone

---

* A 'talk while you walk' has the added bonus of making you feel like someone highly important in a TV drama about a high-flying US law firm, or the White House.

has received the same information as you have, but that isn't always the case.

♦ If change is announced, 'keeping things exactly as they are' is not going to be an option. If you see alternatives, go to your manager with your proposals. The more pragmatic you are, the more your team's involvement will be sought in future.

♦ If you have a team that is going through a tough period at work due to too many changes of plan, you are allowed to acknowledge it with them. Peaks and troughs are normal, and sometimes, when you're in a trough, it is enough to simply recognize it as such, and wait for it to pass.

PART III

FAIRNESS

Chapter 8

The fairness failure

'She's got more cake than me!'
    'No, her slice is bigger!'
    Both my children turn to me and chorus in outrage: 'It's not fair!'

It's safe to say that humans have a very strong, innate sense of fairness. Indeed, your Sunday night dread may be reinforced by a lurking sense that your workplace is not an entirely level playing field.

After *weighing* bits of cake to prove to my children that they're the same size, I once more look to Maslow only to find that fairness is not even mentioned in his hierarchy of needs. Maybe Maslow saw needs as absolute, not relative? But humans are *insanely* relative creatures. Did he never encounter any small children? When I reread his *Theory of Motivation* with a fine-tooth comb, I find that Maslow actually lists fairness, along with freedom and honesty, as overarching prerequisites for all other needs.

Other psychologists have, however, focused more squarely on fairness, and several have emphasized its enormous importance in the workplace. Back in 1963, J. Stacey Adams developed his equity theory, which stated that job motivation is all about feeling like you are being fairly treated compared with others. Adams emphasized the need for balance between what an employee contributes and what they receive in return.

It is important to say that fairness at work is not *equality*, as such, because the workplace is a hierarchy. At work, when we say fairness, we usually mean meritocracy: opportunity and reward relative to merit (a subject we will turn to later). By extension, unfairness is when people are judged for attributes that are irrelevant to how well they perform their roles, or when colleagues of similar merit appear to be more or less valued than they are.

You would think that fairness is reasonably easy for companies to establish and maintain. Compared with, say, the pressure of shareholder return, it's well within the control of a business to act fairly. And yet fairness remains a problem, even in the modern workplace.

Or maybe it's just you, overthinking everything?

It's not just you.

Problems of pay

'Are you paid enough?' asks the employee survey.

'Yes,' writes precisely no one.

'That's the one constant on our survey,' confides one HR manager. Grumbling about salary is a straightforward and universal part of working life: everybody does it.

However, beyond certain base levels, people don't necessarily want more money because of the money itself. Rather, people consider their salary to be a reflection of how they are perceived: are they valued or aren't they? Are they or are they not as good as their peers? In one study, students and staff at the Harvard School of Public Health were asked if they would rather earn $50,000 when everyone else was earning $25,000, or $100,000 when everyone else was earning $200,000 (assuming purchasing power was the same in both examples). Astoundingly, 50% of participants chose the former, even though this left them objectively worse off. We view our pay relative to the pay of others.

Different sectors have different approaches to remuneration. In the United Kingdom the public sector typically offers a fixed salary range within its various grades: a given role pays between X and Y, and that's the end of it. UK private-sector companies have this too – but many then quietly disregard it when they want or need somebody more expensive. In private-sector companies, salary is based on the company's budget for the role and on what you, the candidate, ask for. Employers aim to pay you the minimum required to secure you: typically a bit more than your last salary, and no more.

This is where problems creep in: from the start, pay is anchored not to ability but to what you were able to negotiate at your interview. Employees start in their roles and work alongside their colleagues, with everyone doing a similar role, but their salary remains anchored to their initial sense of self-worth. HR can't exactly cut the salaries of the higher earners and it would cost them a fortune to level things up, so any disparity just ... sits there. Inaction is facilitated by the tacit prohibition of anyone discussing their salary with colleagues.

I speak to one director who got a pay rise only when a higher-paid junior moved under her. 'I couldn't believe what she was earning,' she tells me. 'The junior was in a role with much less responsibility. HR gave me a rise because they knew the manager had to be earning more, but it would never have happened otherwise.'

Your starting salary affects your entire career at a company. Fail to start at the right level and you find yourself stuck behind higher-paid peers for years. As one HR manager tells me, 'If people are brought in low, they are forever playing catch up.' Cost-of-living pay increases, where given, tend to be a percentage of current salary, so they only serve to increase any gap between you and your peers. Many companies, aware of this, have systems to compensate low earners within a grade by awarding above-average annual increases, but the catch-up process is not a quick one.

WHY YOU DREAD WORK

All this hits women particularly hard. Linda Babcock of Carn-
egie Mellon University, co-author of *Women Don't Ask*, reports
that women are four times less likely than men to ask for a pay
rise, and, when they do, they request 30% less than men ask for.
In one study of masters graduates, Babcock found that 57% of
the men had negotiated their starting salary compared with
only 7% of the women, and she observed that this failure alone –
to negotiate the salary of their first job – could cost women half
a million dollars over the course of their career.

When restructures occur, lower-paid employees find themselves automatically on the back foot. One retail buyer tells me:
'I was one of four buyers at senior level. Then a new boss came
in and held a meeting to plan the future structure of the team.
I wasn't invited. Until then I had no idea that, although we all
had the same job title, my colleagues had all been hired at the
grade above me, probably because the salary range for the right
grade was less than they had demanded. They returned from
the meeting having all given themselves more senior job titles –
and having decided I would be reporting into one of them from
then on.'

Gallingly, leaving the business doesn't always help. You are
often handicapped in the next company, too, because new
employers want to know what you earned in your last role. 'Just
lie!' suggests my husband, somewhat concerningly. But given
that it's one of the things HR is likely to check in your references,
bluffing is a high-risk strategy. (My advice to people is to instead
anchor the conversation around the salary they are seeking.)

There are, however, glimmers of light. Since 2017, in New
York and in some other US states, it has been illegal for an interviewer to ask your current salary. This is great news, and we must
encourage the practice to spread outside the United States.

It is safe to say that people care about fairness relative to
their colleagues, but there is also a second strand to fairness in
remuneration: are you being paid fairly relative to the market
itself? One almost invisible practice penalizes the most faithful,

long-serving and expert members of an organization: it is known as the loyalty penalty.

The loyalty penalty

Miriam, a CRM support analyst for an energy company, is in her late twenties. Quiet and diligent, she has gained deep knowledge of the company's systems over the years, and her colleagues love the way she spots details they might have missed. When a new manager asks for a list of his team's salaries, he's shocked: Miriam is earning far less than her peers. HR robustly defends the disparity: Miriam was promoted internally from a junior role in the call centre – she's lucky to have moved up. Miriam has received above-average salary increases over the years: 10% for the initial move out of the call centre, 7% the next year and 8% in the last financial year. Compared with the inflationary increases of 2–3% that her colleagues have received, Miriam's increases have been among the highest in the whole company!

Her manager argues back. The percentage increase is the wrong metric because her base rate was so low. Miriam should be aligned with her peers immediately. The market rate for someone in Miriam's role, with her level of experience, is roughly double her current salary. HR explains that the business caps salary increases for internal moves at 10%. The conversation is over.

This is the loyalty penalty in action.

There's a saying in the world of property: 'You make your money when you buy.' In a similar vein, at work, you make your money when you move – move companies, that is, not roles. This is true for a number of reasons. Internal candidates are, by definition, already in situ, whereas external candidates need to be lured away from their current employer. Internal candidates often lack direct experience of their new role, so are hired based on potential rather than experience. But companies also get tangled up in the narrow logic of paying the minimum they need

WHY YOU DREAD WORK

to secure a given individual, rather than paying the going rate for the role.

One impact of the loyalty penalty is to unwittingly perpetuate the gender pay gap. Since 2017, companies in the United Kingdom have had to report on the pay difference between men and women. Unfortunately, the pay gap only has to be reported in overall terms, not by grade or by role. (It is also worth noting that while gender pay gap reporting is mandatory in Britain, there is not yet any legal obligation to make a plan to address it.) The reason that many UK companies give for their shocking gender pay gaps – data from the Office for National Statistics for 2020 shows an average discrepancy of 15.5%, and ten sectors with gaps exceeding 30% – is therefore that, regrettably, women tend to occupy the more junior roles. Companies explain that they will 'help women aim higher', or words to that effect, pointing to their new women's network and their mentoring scheme. But policies that limit internal pay rises unwittingly scupper these efforts. Those who start in those tricky junior roles are never going to catch up.

Gemma Clarke, a technical support manager, thought she was doing OK because for every internal move she would get a pay rise. But, she tells me, 'One day I overheard a colleague on the phone. She was offering a new recruit, a junior, the same salary I was earning as a senior.' Gemma asked the HR department to benchmark her salary against that of her peers, and she was reluctantly given a 20% pay rise. Gemma says: 'My boss said, "This is a whopping pay rise – I hope you're happy!" His tone was affronted – I had made a fuss about money. I bit my lip and thought, don't you mean, you've had a massive bargain for two years?'

As one headhunter tells me, 'Companies get away with the disparity because no one talks about money.' He tells me of employment contracts that stipulate that you must not discuss your salary with colleagues. All this conveniently puts the onus on the team member: unless Gemma overhears a rare conversation about money, she has to somehow flag a discrepancy of which she is unaware and for which she can present no evidence. There is an inbuilt imbalance of information.

A company may practice other salary-limiting tactics, such as making employees feel awkward about asking for more money when they are given extra responsibility. 'Not now,' they reply, sounding vaguely amused. 'We'll assess it at performance review time.' By that point the employee has already been doing the job for six months, so the manager knows full well they will work for the current rate.

Or perhaps the employee's manager is on their side and tries to get them the top end of the scale for an internal promotion but is persuaded by HR to go for a rate at the low end 'to give them space to grow'. I'll leave it to you to contemplate how grateful you would feel for this extra space.

The great irony here is that those who are promoted internally are likely to be a company's strongest employees: after all, they shone brightly enough to gain promotion. So you get a situation where the strongest may be paid the least within their peer group, just because they came from within the business. If that isn't twisted logic, what is?

In all this, there is also a longer-term risk. Companies only secure an employee for as long as that employee believes they are getting a fair deal. At some point the employee is likely to realize two things: first, that colleagues in the same role are earning substantially more than them; and second, that they can get this higher amount by moving elsewhere. So they leave, taking all their accumulated knowledge and potential with them. The company is left with the hefty cost of replacing them, which, depending on the sector, can easily cost a year's salary or more.

Some companies do have a policy of raising a salary to market level – but only on production of a written job offer from another business. This is a distinctly high-risk retention strategy. During the interview process somewhere new, employees make a moral and time-based investment in the new company. They assess their fit with their potential new boss and colleagues. It's like buying a house: what could be perceived as a neutral financial transaction is actually highly emotional. By the time an offer is made, they have imagined themselves living there and mentally bought a new sofa. Companies should not assume that employees will be retained simply because of the safety of the familiar, especially when they have clearly been taken for a ride.

Nikolai Balzer, head of governance at LMA Recruitment, agrees: 'About 70% of people who try to leave, and then stay purely for money, tend to leave anyway within seven to eight months. Because the move wasn't ultimately just about money. And by then the trust is gone.'

One headhunter I speak to takes a different view: 'Why voluntarily hand people more cash? If they leave, they can just hire someone else.' Balzer groans over his coffee when I tell him this: 'It's not that simple. Companies only realize what they've lost once the employee has left. People come to me asking for a new employee – often they literally say, "We'd like a new Alex, please" – and I have to tell them, it's not possible for that salary. Typically the line manager is incredibly frustrated – usually they wanted to give them a pay rise but they were told there was no budget.'

In all this, the company has not broken any official clause in its contract of employment with employees. However, there is also an unspoken contract alongside the formal, written terms and conditions of employment: an implicit contract of trust that companies will do the decent thing when no one is looking. This is where issues such as pay unfairness really sting – the natural imbalance of information makes it more, not less, necessary to be fair.

When employees feel they've been treated unfairly, the decay in trust is swift. People are likely to become disgruntled and make less effort. In one 2015 study reported in the *Personality and Social Psychology Bulletin*, researchers found that employees who had previously trusted their organization but had then had that trust broken displayed the biggest decline in commitment to their company compared with the average worker. Employees who felt they had been treated unfairly were more than twice as likely to feel angry (27% versus 13%) and not to feel proud to work for their organization (75% versus 35%).

People don't generally quit on the spot, but the unspoken contract has been broken, leaving behind a more world-weary, purely transactional one.

In the case of salary discrepancy, this may eventually produce the unwanted effect of pay-related performance, as opposed to performance-related pay. If employees know their salary is low relative to their peers – the crunch point is anything less than 80% of the peer amount for any sustained period of time – they will dial back their effort.

Employees may even feel unfairness at a physical level. One study of more than 19,000 Swedish employees by the University of East Anglia and Stockholm University found an increased risk of sick days among employees who felt unfairly treated at work. In another research study, economist and academic Armin Falk found that people's heart rate variability – an early risk factor for coronary heart disease – increased when they felt they were not fairly paid for conducting routine tasks. When the researchers analysed a large data set, the results also bore this out more broadly: perceptions of unfair pay correlated with an increased risk of long-term cardiovascular health issues.

The wider market expects employees to be treated fairly, too. This implicit expectation of fairness feeds into something else that is intangible but that helps drive the bottom line: a company's brand. A strong brand exists largely via perception and cannot be pinned down in spreadsheet form, yet it has immense financial value.

Of course companies no longer own their brand communications in the way they used to, because any consumer who chooses to do so can broadcast their view on social media. This can be a bonus for the workforce because companies are now held to account much more by the public than they used to be. A recent example of this came in 2020 after part of the supply chain at fashion retailer Boohoo was reported to be paying workers less than the minimum wage – leading to an outcry from consumers on social media.

Meanwhile, job candidates are another group who display a keen eye for fairness. Companies such as Glassdoor bring the inside out, and it is not unusual for prospective employees to look up a company's gender pay gap or check out their policy on flexible working before accepting a position.

Eventually, if an environment feels unfair, some of those within the company will simply leave. One study reported in the *Harvard Business Review* found that employees who had experienced unfairness were 60% more likely to have sought a new job elsewhere in the previous six months. Meanwhile, Andrew Chamberlain, director of research and chief economist at Glassdoor, has observed in his firm's data that people almost always leave one company for another that has a better culture. And those latter organizations retain staff better, too: each star on a company's Glassdoor rating positively impacts their retention rate by 4%.

It is rare that the financial cost of a short-term attitude to salary is measured. It is easy to save money by underpaying loyal staff – the P&L bears this out – but the hidden costs of lost productivity, retention and trust go unremarked.

So, fair pay is indisputably important – but what about getting into a company in the first place, or being able to progress once you are there?

Chapter 9

Who gets in – and who moves up

The human desire for fair treatment should dovetail beautifully with a core concept of the modern workplace: that of meritocracy. In theory, a meritocracy means that no one should ever dread Monday morning – not on the grounds of unfairness, at least. If reward is based on merit alone, then workplaces are fair, because everyone – in, out, high or low – is in the right place. So why did the inventor of the word, the sociologist Michael Young, intend it as a negative term?

Meritocracy perhaps makes the most sense in the context of what came before it. Before the concept of meritocracy – at least in the United Kingdom – the feudal system or your social class defined you at birth, so there was a certain inevitability to where you ended up. If it was hard to move up the social or economic scale, it was hardly your fault – that was just the way it was. Helping you swallow this bitter pill was a strong religious narrative that your worldly status did not reflect the state of your soul. Every man was equal under God. Aristocrats shouldn't think that their elevated status bestowed any moral virtue on them, and the peasant did not need to despair, for the meek shall inherit the earth.

The concept of meritocracy throws aside those historical structures determined by birth. Finally! A system based on what you bring to the table. Surely fairness is *baked in*.

But meritocracy as a concept is far from simple, and this is where Young sounded caution. Unlike the structures it upended, meritocracy assigns virtue to the act of reaching the top of the tree. This gives it a self-congratulatory nature absent from the feudal or class systems, in which everyone knew that their position was an accident of birth. After all, if your ascent is self-determined, and you reach the top, it must be because your own actions merited it. You must be fantastic! However, flip the coin and meritocracy shifts any blame for failure onto those who fail. After all, if meritocracy means a level playing field, then any failure must be your own fault.*

The second issue with meritocracy is when you realize, somewhat uncomfortably, that the definition of merit, and decisions regarding who has earned it, are made by those at the top. This risks skewing the contest in favour of whatever those in charge happen to value – an MBA degree, perhaps. Any subjectivity in that definition and suddenly it's looking a little self-reinforcing, and a lot less fair.

Recruitment or advancement within a company are where the concept of meritocracy is most relevant and most tested. Obviously, the best way to gain a balanced workforce is a hot topic. Into the mix comes plenty of debate about topics such as whether positive discrimination is necessary or is in itself unfair, and how to eliminate bias. Meanwhile, traditional definitions of merit are being examined and found lacking. Recently, for example, the emphasis placed on having a university degree has come under renewed fire, with critics such as journalist and author David Goodhart arguing that it has become an overrated, ineffective and expensive barrier to entry.

Bias is a book in itself – and a delicate path to tread – but one of the more intriguing aspects of recruiting staff is the rigidity of

---

* The marvellous book *How to Lose Friends and Alienate People* by Toby Young, Michael Young's son, briefly discusses the impact of this meritocratic ideal on American society.

what constitutes a good CV. Let's look at one particular aspect: the idea that you must not take a break.

What happens if you stop?

One of the most fundamental causes of work-related dread has to be feeling trapped – in this case, to keep following your current path. Perhaps you never intended to get into your current profession, but now it is all you can get hired to do. Or, your job is fine, but you want or need a break.

When on a Sunday night we think to ourselves, 'Why are we doing this?' there are many reasons: financial and habitual ones, among others. Yet another reason is fear. What if we stop, or try to change paths, and then lose what we have built up? What if we're not allowed back on the treadmill?

This is not an unwarranted concern: a break in your career *does* impact your ability to get back on. And this is a fundamentally misjudged and unfair aspect of working life.

The rationale trotted out across the board – so much so that it has become unthinkingly accepted – is that if you take a break, you lose knowledge and competence. Recruitment expert Nikolai Balzer agrees that the perception is real: 'A break of one to two years is doable; however, it gets harder every six months you have off. Companies definitely place greater value on those already in employment.'

Why is this idea so ingrained? Does the fact that another company already wants a candidate make them, perversely, more desirable in the eyes of recruiting managers? As Balzer tells me, 'Sometimes, people need up-to-date knowledge of regulations, or the latest certificates. Training budgets are being cut, so if there are qualified candidates, companies are simply more likely to take one of those.'

Yet the perception that 'a break is bad' extends across all industries, not just those requiring regularly updated qualifications. Take the classic break of maternity leave, something with such a damaging impact that it has its own name: the mother-hood penalty. In a 2019 study spanning the United States and Northern Europe, researchers found that a mother's earnings fall sharply after their first child and, even after a decade, do not recover. In the United States and the United Kingdom, the net earnings penalty was 40%.

Tracy Jordan is one individual who had to overcome the impact of a career break. A VP in an investment bank by the age of thirty, Tracy was sent to Chicago with her husband and two young children to set up the organization's derivatives account-ing team. Once established, her role was to remain in Chicago, but Tracy wanted to move back to London so she took voluntary redundancy to spend a year with her children. The year turned into several. Tracy had a third child, started her own business and worked extensively for charities.

When Tracy tried to get back into banking she hit a wall. She tells me: 'When my youngest child was settled at school, I called the recruitment consultants who tried to headhunt me before my career break, but I was told I was either underqualified or overqualified. My work during my time off counted for nothing: I was told I would need to take a more junior role to get back in.'

The days of expecting a candidate to work nonstop until they retire should be long gone, yet the market still looks down on candidates who've had a break from full-time employment. This means plenty of people who could be strengthening your organization are, instead, at home getting really good at making sourdough bread. If they're not linked in, they're locked out.

When somebody wants to return to work, no matter how valiant their attempts at highlighting transferable skills gained during their time out, recruiters are pretty adept at spotting the career break disguised as something else on a CV:

09/20–09/21. Project manager for high-quality residential property renovation.
[*Recruiter thinks: got some bifold doors put in.*]

Or perhaps a beleaguered parent retrofits their time off to the language of the workplace:

09/20–09/21. Career break to raise my son. Delivered son on time and on budget with skill set in excess of Early Years Foundation literacy and numeracy requirements. Effectively managed household budget. Developed strong communication and networking skills.
[*Recruiter thinks: I need a cup of tea.*]

We should be striving to get to this situation:

09/20–09/21. Career break to raise my son.
[*Recruiter thinks: fair enough.*]

Frankly, change is long overdue because many industries – even technology and finance – fail to move as quickly as popular myth would have you believe. Time off does not turn you into a useless husk; your previous ability totally gone. 'Fast-paced industry change' is the phrase used to terrify new mothers in the United Kingdom, who are made to believe that they'll return to their old employer after maternity leave, quaking, to find a near-incomprehensible world of technological brilliance. In reality, they find that Matt still hasn't fixed that bug in the software and those weird sweets from someone's foreign holiday are still in the middle of the desk. It is true that people's *confidence* suffers during time out, but this is different to any loss of actual ability. If we erased this myth of time out making people ineffective, their confidence would quickly return.

Moreover, why is relentless, uninterrupted work the only way to demonstrate one's ability? An uninterrupted work history arguably shows dedication, but while our parents' generation was raised to believe that loyalty was the quality most valued by employers, this is no longer the case: what today's employers really need is flexibility.

'It's an unfounded fear,' agrees Nikolai Balzer. 'People think time off shows that you have prioritized something other than work in the past, and that you might do it again.' Surely, we agree, it's *less* likely: there are only ever a finite number of children that need raising or parents that need care.

Sometimes it feels like sour grapes. 'I worked without a break for the last twenty years,' think those in employment: 'Why should this person get to take time out and then swan back in?' Studying the related issue of part-time work, Joan Williams, a law professor from the University of California, has indeed observed this kind of attitude. While flexible workplace policies undoubtedly exist, what matters is not the policy but the personal circumstances of the person enforcing it. Williams writes:

> The National Study of the Changing Workforce found that supervisors with employed spouses provided more job-related and family support than those married to homemakers. Meanwhile a study by the Families and Work Institute found that the bosses women found most difficult to deal with have wives who do not work outside the home.

Whatever the official policy, the conversation about flexible working is a difficult one because it represents a direct challenge to the choices made by those managers in their own family lives.

The more closely the current system is examined, the more perverse it appears, because it's only *selectively* judgemental. Time off to travel is fine, because hotshot types do it: it's seen as a growth experience. But time off to care for an elderly relative is penalized because it is low-status work, and you could have hired someone else to do it.

In a highly unscientific experiment I ask a few interviewees in private-sector jobs how they would explain a career break to a prospective employer if they had to choose between (i) saying they'd received such a large windfall of company shares that they hadn't needed to work for a bit or (ii) that they had cared for an elderly relative. People winced as they admitted the windfall story would sound better. The windfall story makes you sound successful and lucky. Quitting your job to look after a relative shows that you value family over career: not something you advertise in more cut-throat corporate environments. If you don't know the (fictional) interviewer's viewpoint, why take the risk? In the workplace, love is not a recognized currency.

In all this, the impact is likely to be totally invisible. And yet dismissing the CVs of those who've had time out unwittingly impoverishes a company. The candidate poached direct from a competitor is probably exhausted and needs a month off, but they won't ever get one, making it more likely that they'll burn out while working for the new company. In contrast, the career-breaker is well rested and hungry to dive back in. Returners are also highly motivated to prove themselves: recruits are likely to repay their new company many times over in dedication. Chief product officer Spiros Theodossiou agrees: 'People who've had time out represent huge untapped potential to employers. The people who return after a career break are often incredibly driven and committed.'

Tracy Jordan finally got a break when she got talking to one of the other mothers by the side of her son's rugby pitch. The other mother happened to work in banking, and she promptly introduced Tracy to her in-house recruiter, who proposed an initial contract role. Tracy then worked her way back up to senior director within the minimum possible timeframe, before moving on to senior roles in other companies.

Career-breakers are great people to have around in a crisis: noticeably less panicky than their hoop-jumping, rule-abiding compatriots. The live system has gone down and your biggest client is on the phone, shouting? That's fine. It's all fixable. There's nothing like having weathered a year of sleepless nights with a newborn or caring for a dying parent to give you a helpful chunk of perspective.

WHY YOU DREAD WORK

Your career is only part of your life, after all. Knowing this doesn't somehow make you less effective, or less motivated: it makes you *wise*.

Invisible rules

'I know – I couldn't believe it!' Sabina Amini, a helpdesk manager, tells me over Zoom. Even on a grainy connection, I can see her rolling her eyes.

Assuming you get into a company in the first place, there is another aspect to fairness: who gets to move up the ranks?

Back in 2014 Sabina was just back from maternity leave when the head of her department mentioned in a group call that the manager of a parallel team was leaving. The new vacancy was perfect for Sabina: she was already managing a team, and she had seven years of relevant experience. This team had a few more people in it, but that would make it an ideal step up. But in the same breath the head of department continued: 'Rehan's taking on the role – he'll start in a few weeks.'

'I liked Rehan,' says Sabina, 'but he was less experienced, and wasn't even based in the same office as his team-to-be, whereas I was right there.'

In private Sabina asked her manager why they hadn't opened the role up to interview, and she watched as it dawned on him that he had made an error. 'He said honestly, "Oh – I didn't think of you," and asked apologetically if I wanted him to hold interviews for the role.' Sabina said no. 'Maybe I should have insisted, but what was the point? I didn't want a grudge interview – they had already offered Rehan the role and told everyone.'

Sabina reflects on what went wrong: 'I was really busy during that period, and kept my head down. I'd recently been off on maternity leave. I did as much work as I could get through, but that was all I had time for. Rehan was a great relationship-builder. I think that's what happened – no senior people really knew what I could do.'

At school and university the rules are clear for everyone: work hard and you will be rewarded. Effort, application and dedication are the things that are valued. Jump through all the right hoops – get good exam results and a good degree, do some voluntary work somewhere exotic – and you'll eventually get your first job. So far, so good. And for a while in your new workplace, the rules remain straightforward: how well can you do your role, and how much volume can you manage?

As you scale the ranks, however, the rules quietly change. Suddenly, promotions depend more on networking, on your presentation ability and sphere of influence, and on other intangible merits. No one tells you there are invisible hoops ahead: you're supposed to *just know*. For the first time, those hoops are also subjective and hard to measure. As the first in her family to go to university and to work in a corporate role, Sabina didn't even know the hoops were there.

The diligence you showed in your twenties still makes you indispensable, but it doesn't get you promoted. It gets you … well, more work. The sense of betrayal can be acute. This even has its own name: Tiara syndrome, a concept coined by Carol Frohlinger and Deborah Kolb, the founders of Negotiating Women Inc. This is the belief, from women in particular, that if you keep your head down and work hard, someone will notice your talents, promptly place a tiara on your head and reward you. But in fact the reverse is true. When weighing up two candidates, who is a manager likely to choose: the person who they could lift out really easily from their current role, or the person so indispensable that it would take three people to replace them? Jen Edwards, head of product for a media company, agrees: 'Sometimes the hardest workers are not the people who end up at the top – they're too integral to their current team.'

Promotions therefore go to those who have mastered the invisible rules of this new landscape: how much you are known by the people who matter, how confidently you speak, and how keenly you seek high-status projects.

When I coach people (both male and female), I always tell them something I picked up from the fantastically titled *Nice Girls Don't Get the Corner Office* by Lois P. Frankel: give yourself permission to 'waste' 5% of your day talking to people. It's really not a waste – it just feels that way to the diligent. That time building relationships may be the most valuable you spend at work.

It's tempting to see the new rules themselves as unfair, but they're ultimately logical: leadership *is* less about being an individual contributor and more about building relationships, influencing people and securing resources. People have to be ready to step away from doing and delegate work to others. The unfairness lies in the invisibility of the hoops: many people are simply unaware of the dramatic shift in the skills that they need to demonstrate.

So, the choice of who gets into a company, and who moves up, can be contentious territory, fraught with invisible rules. Don't stop working or you'll be judged! If you want a promotion, demonstrate these skills! Perhaps you only learn these things the hard way, and enjoy ample opportunity to kick yourself for past mistakes. Or perhaps you are all too aware of what is needed. In this case, you have a decision to make: will you be your natural self, regardless, or mould yourself to what a company appears to want?

Chapter 10

Please wear a mask

The word performance has a double meaning: the action of performing a certain function, and also that of putting on an act. A 'high-performance culture' means that people are good at doing what needs to be done. But how many of them are also projecting something other than their natural self?

Progression through the ranks does not always feel fair. So, at some point employees learn, possibly the hard way, that they need to offer an organization what it wants. If that is not their true, unvarnished self, what do they do? Well, they adopt a professional mask of some kind. In one Deloitte survey, 61% of respondents admitted to covering up who they are in front of their colleagues – this included 45% of straight white men.

Of course, for all the recent buzz around 'bringing yourself to work' or authentic leadership, untrammelled authenticity is a tricky thing. We take for granted that authenticity is something to strive for at all costs, but in his book *The Weirdest People in the World*,* evolutionary biologist Joseph Henrich describes the drive for authenticity as a Western phenomenon, remarking that other cultures are far more tolerant of people behaving differently depending on who they're with. The aim to be ourselves across differing contexts is laudable, but it is perhaps

---

* The 'weird' of Henrich's title stands for Western, educated, industrialized, rich and democratic.

overly individualistic. After all, authenticity – with its air of 'This is me! Take it or leave it!' – implies you value your own perspective over the needs of those around you. Sometimes people do need to suppress unhelpful emotions or project confidence: for the good of their team, for example. Martina King, CEO of the artificial intelligence company FeatureSpace, tells me: 'I try to be open and vulnerable. Authenticity is powerful. I will give people the facts. But people also need your confidence. You have to be strong for your team, and find that inner and outer strength.'

On occasion you may need to assume confidence over a longer period, in order to grow into a new version of yourself. In my first proper job, fresh out of university at twenty-two, there was an awful lot I didn't know about work. I assumed that working life involved a simple and fair equation: your real self + some skills = a fairly determined amount of money. I also assumed that those higher up from me were there because they had some special combination of attributes that I simply didn't possess.

I wore no mask at all: it didn't occur to me to do so. There was no distinction between my true self and my work self. I avoided stretch projects like the plague. More work? Ha! That was for idiots! If I was annoyed, I looked annoyed. If I was sleepy, I looked sleepy.* I believed this to be showing admirable integrity: in reality, I was essentially unpromotable. I did eventually advance into more senior roles but this was in spite of, rather than because of, my outlook.

Fast forward a few years, and I find myself in a new, more senior, role in a new organization. I attempt something akin to an experiment: I decide to reinvent myself professionally. Belatedly, something has hit me: the people above me in the organization are essentially *the same as me*, they just believe they can do it. So, in a kind of curious social experiment, I do the

---

* I apologize to the product manager in whose product launch I actually dozed off. It was before I actually became a product manager myself and would no doubt have this effect on other people.

things I've observed senior people doing: I take care never to seem stressed. I appear confident. I comment in performance reviews that I am ready for more responsibility. And it works: I am promoted and gain a job title so long that it won't fit on my business cards.

I also decide after my memorable urge to flee the stage at the enormous conference in Brussels that I want to become better at public speaking. In a workshop run by the actress Matilda Thorpe I learn something revelatory: you can *choose* how you feel while presenting. It is a lightbulb moment: for years I have tried to master my nerves, trying to stop them from owning me, when actually I haven't realized that I own them. I can simply choose to act as though I am not nervous. After that, wherever I am in the world – from Barcelona to Vegas – I still nervously rehearse in my hotel room while ironing my dress, but then I get on stage and say, with a smile, how great it is to see everyone.

Being up on stage without running away is initially exhausting: there is a big divide, after all, between my authentic self (happiest on the sofa with a book) and my work self (capable human). Yet after a while I realize something unexpected: I have genuinely become a more competent speaker. In pushing myself to do things that make me uncomfortable, I've accidentally become the person I've been pretending to be. I only learn afterwards of the Eleanor Roosevelt quotation, 'You gain courage and confidence from doing the things you think you cannot do.' I learn that 'fake it until you make it' is not always a facade: it can be a genuine tutor.

Then again, my professional transformation was also exhausting. Off the top of my head, here are a few of the things I have learned to do over the years in order to appear more credible:

- Speak early in meetings.
- Don't tilt your head when listening (feminine gesture).
- Sit right at the front to make it clear you are in charge.

- Never phrase statements as a question.
- To avoid getting talked over in meetings, make yourself more imposing by standing up and walking around while you speak.
- Don't say 'just' or 'maybe'.
- Don't write notes. (I can never manage this one, as an inveterate scribbler.)
- Never offer to make tea. (I also can't manage this one. People need tea.)
- Never admit you don't know.
- Never say you can't do something.
- Don't laugh or smile too much.
- Wear make-up, but not too much.
- Never sit with one leg tucked underneath you (another feminine gesture).
- Dress consistently, above all other considerations: whatever your outfit does, it should never surprise.
- Go first during team exercises so you look proactive. (This one gives you the distinct advantage of being done first, so you can relax afterwards.)
- Highlight your accomplishments in one-to-one meetings with your manager because otherwise they will not notice the work you do.
- Say frequently that you're ready for the next step, because people will take you at your own reckoning.
- Spend time networking or face the consequences.

Oh, and take up physical space in a meeting room. This works wonderfully if you are a man and can spreadeagle your arms and legs, slowly swivelling your chair as you opine on this quarter's sales numbers, leading people to think to themselves: 'Ah, Jeff – assertive go-getter.' This works less well if you are a woman, whose only physical equivalent is to spread her possessions across multiple seats. This just makes people think: 'Ah, Helen – scatterer-of-random-objects.'

Occasionally I wonder what I could have fitted in my head instead of remembering all that.

And the list is *still*, basically: 'Act more like a man.'

Other women who have scaled the ranks at work roll their eyes when I talk about this: some have been wearing their masks for twenty years or more. They're exhausted. Charlotte Webb is a C-level executive, for goodness' sake, and still she says, 'Oh - the facade – I've done it for years. I've only just grown enough self-worth to take it off. It's to protect myself. We do it to ourselves. You feel the need to mirror what's around you.'

Of course, organizational cultures vary enormously according to their male–female mix and the sector they're in. My background is in technology companies, in technical roles, which means I'm often the only woman in the room. My husband is utterly baffled by the above list, but then again he works in TV, where he tells me he is expected to be creative and wacky.

Another pervasive mask is that of extroversion. Anyone who has ever wondered why they are quite so exhausted when they get home needs to read *Quiet* by Susan Cain. Cain explains that, in essence, introverts can do any job they put their mind to, but if their job demands an extrovert persona, they should expect to be more tired than their extrovert peers at the end of the day.

The dominance of the loud and assertive in meetings and in decision-making means that acting more extroverted than you really are is simply a necessity for many people – something to be managed. It's all a bit tedious, given that there's no correlation between being loud and being right. While seeking a variable that could predict team effectiveness, Google's Project Aristotle looked at the extroversion of team members but found that it was insignificant.

When decision making is dominated by the most verbal thinkers, those who prefer to reflect on a problem are often simply not heard, and the culture of the loud becomes a self-reinforcing spiral. It risks becoming the definition of success in your company. Once, at interview with a well-known Big Tech company, I was shown to a room with a whiteboard wall, given a marker pen and told: 'Monetize [highly popular free product].' The task was to instantly think of a viable plan and present it persuasively to my interviewer, visualizing my thought process by writing and drawing confidently as I went. Thanks to various forums dedicated to the company's dastardly interview process, I was well prepared for something like this, but I was also very conscious of the fact that this wasn't my natural way of working. I preferred to reflect quietly, scribble a few notes alone somewhere, and then come up with a proposal. Later, I questioned the approach with the recruitment team, who explained that the company valued fast, devolved decision making. I had to wonder: how good are those fast decisions? If you only value the most verbal and assertive people, do you not occasionally miss great ideas?

Of course, no organization would intentionally force their employees into a mask. Let me be clear: we put them on ourselves, to fit in, or to cover up that we don't feel good enough. Yet so much mask-wearing at work feels necessary: driven by a sense that what is valued is different from what we naturally offer. Masks have their roots in insecurity: if you're not sure of yourself, armour is useful. Either way masks are exhausting, with the constant dissonance between how you would act naturally and how you feel you should behave.

How do I feel about my mask-wearing? I definitely grew professionally but I also wonder what I lost along the way. I probably deprived myself of genuine connections, which means that I isolated myself much more than I needed to.

The irony is that there are probably tons of people all wearing masks at work because they think it is what they should be doing. Christin Munsch, an assistant professor of sociology at the University of Connecticut, ran a research study on 'pluralistic ignorance'. Loosely speaking, this is the term for when an individual privately dislikes a certain norm but mistakenly thinks everyone else must be fine with it. Surveying US workers,

Munsch and her team found that masculinity contest cultures (referenced in chapter 3) were prone to pluralistic ignorance. This led to reduced job satisfaction and lower engagement while also impacting mental health and relationships outside work. Another danger is that those adopting a professional mask over-shoot the mark, acting in a more extrovert or assertive manner than they actually need to. This unwittingly reinforces the idea that it's the only way for others to behave, too.

If you do drop the mask, you rapidly find that other people feel the same. At a recent technology conference I heard a very eloquent data scientist speak on a panel. She was quite daz-zling, and yet she told the audience that she often felt like she wasn't good enough, to the extent that she kept an email folder of praise for her work to make herself feel better. Now that, I thought to myself, sounded exactly like the kind of nonsense that I would do. During the dreaded networking lunch after-wards, a young woman who worked at the BBC came up to me. We'd both been in the audience of the panel discussion and I mentioned how staggering it was that the data scientist – some-one so apparently composed – had expressed such self-doubt. The woman said to me: 'I had to pluck up the courage to come and talk to you!' It's still all too easy to look around and see only apparent certainty.

Burnout

Have you ever done a Myers–Briggs personality test? I've done several at various points in my career. At one point – when I was right in the middle of assuming the mantle of a polished, extro-vert leader – I recall that my peers and I all came out as ENTJs or similar: that is, classic gung-ho executive types.

Years later I decide to hold an offsite workshop and do the test with my own lovely team. There are a number of introverts in the group, so I want us to discuss how to make sure every-one's voice is heard. My own result swings wildly, to introverted.

I'm not that surprised: at some point I've cast off my mask. Perhaps I wanted to lose it before it ate into my face.

Some people, though, don't feel they can unmask, and a sense of dissonance continues. People describe the sense of a gap between their natural self and the expectations of their organization. Depending on the attribute being masked, between 60% and 73% of respondents in one Deloitte study felt that covering up was detrimental to their sense of self.

Sometimes the faultlines just keep widening, and dread may turn into burnout, which was recognized as an occupational phenomenon by the World Health Organization in 2010.

Dr Judith Mohring describes the symptoms of burnout as a vicious cycle. First people become more self-critical, and rate their own abilities lower. Then this anxiety makes them slower, less accurate and less decisive. And eventually people start to withdraw – while the tasks pile up. 'People need to recognize that spiral and rest,' says Mohring. 'However, they probably don't recognize the need to pause – and even if they did, they would not think they deserved it.'

Burnout can stem from too much workload, but people can generally deal with a large volume of work as long as their role fits with their natural values and working style. Dr Christina Maslach, a social psychologist, has studied the phenomenon since the 1970s. Together with Susan E. Jackson of Rutgers University, she created the respected Maslach Burnout Inventory. The pair's findings pointed to six factors: workload, certainly, but also control, reward, community, fairness and values. The executive we met earlier who had been signed off on stress leave tells me: 'For me, it's the constant persona that, one day, just gets too much. They say "be authentic" at my workplace now, but it's just lip service. You go to work and have to constantly make sure you get heard, and say the right things, but it's not who I am. It was a definite factor in my burnout.'

One common thread in workplace dread and risk of burnout is a negative relationship with your immediate boss, because it is such a pivotal relationship. When I call Parul Sharma, a senior director at LexisNexis Risk Solutions, to talk about fairness, she emphasizes that her positive experience of her workplace comes from her immediate leader. 'My employer really lives its values,' she tells me over Zoom from California. 'I say that because of my immediate team. I trust my boss explicitly. It's been five years and he still lives up to that trust.'

Others find that if they have the boss's support, they can tolerate a much greater workload than would otherwise be feasible. One business analyst is fairly typical. He tells me, 'I can put up with a ton of workload and politics, as long as I know my manager has my back, and that I can go to her if I get stuck.'

An unsupportive relationship with your manager, however, can feel traumatic, and is a major cause of Sunday night dread. McKinsey reports that 75% of Americans say that the most stressful aspect of their working day is their boss.

Years ago, I experienced an instructive exchange in a performance review. I had accomplished lots of complex work without asking my manager for assistance, and I was really proud of what my team and I had managed to achieve. However, I had experienced one really big issue that I couldn't resolve because it was outside my sphere of control. The conversation in my review went like this:

> **Manager** (in a critical tone): You needed help with X and this took up my time.
> **Me:** I suppose I see the role of manager as someone you can go to if you need help.
> **Manager:** At a certain level you're supposed to decide things by yourself.
> **Me:** I guess that makes me feel quite alone.

Here, I hesitate. I'm pretty certain my boss then told me, 'You are alone.' Did he really say that? Maybe I just felt it? I still recall the gut punch as it sunk in that I was on my own. Either way: sometimes it doesn't matter what role you are in, whether you are a junior or a senior something-or-other, you simply need some help. Paul Polman of Unilever once said, 'Most leaders delegate complexity downward; I feel it should be just the opposite. You should delegate complexity upward.'

There is a reason why the better employee surveys include a question on whether you can go to your manager with problems. A climate where individuals have to manage major challenges alone may help them develop, or it may be isolating.

For some, dreading work hits at the moments when they feel the greatest gap between their own values and those of the company. Making people redundant is often a key moment of crisis. A leader will have invested in building a sense of team, but is then asked to shake its foundations. One C-level executive still sounds pained as he recalls having to make an entire team redundant to show a saving in the P&L for that year. 'It was my lowest point in the role,' he tells me. 'I left shortly afterwards.'

Mel MacIntyre, a business coach, had a similar experience. The final straw was taking her father to hospital for a big operation, then going into work where she had to make several people redundant. As she told Emine Saner of *The Guardian in 2021*, 'I woke up one day, and there was nothing left to draw on.'

The impact of burnout makes for unnerving reading. It has been associated in research studies with neurological damage, impaired cognitive function and other health problems. One Israeli research study reported in the journal *Psychosomatic Medicine* followed nearly 9,000 otherwise-healthy employees. It found that those in the top 20% for burnout symptoms had a 79% greater risk of being diagnosed with coronary heart disease – not decades later, but within the study's 3.4-year follow-up period.

Jock Busuttil, founder of Product People Ltd, tells me: 'Once, before leaving a job, I went to see a doctor because I genuinely didn't know why I felt so terrible – physically and mentally. The doctor wrote down a prescription and handed me the bit of paper. The prescription said, "Get a new job."'

This is precisely what Mel McIntyre did. She quit her job, spent a year travelling and then set up her own company to help others avoid burnout.

Burnout is so damaging because it often involves a gap between how we act at work and what we believe to be our essential selves. But what can be done to close this gap? And are companies structured to care?

Chapter 11

Making fairness fundamental

In the discussion of fairness at work, there is perhaps a final, awkward truth. In his book *The Road to Character*, the columnist David Brooks divides human virtues into two kinds: résumé virtues and eulogy virtues. He writes:

> The résumé virtues are the ones you list on your résumé, the skills that you bring to the job market and that contribute to external success. The eulogy virtues are deeper. They're the virtues that get talked about at your funeral – the ones that exist at the core of your being – whether you are kind, brave, honest or faithful.

Eulogy virtues are the things other people say about you, not the things you say about yourself.

The issue is that companies don't necessarily value what you bring to the table – or, at least, not the eulogy characteristics that you value in your personal life, such as effort, empathy or loyalty. Imagine you struggle hard at something and it doesn't work out. Your gut reaction might be, 'But I tried so hard!' That should count for something – but a company doesn't care if you tried: it is set up only to reward results. Also (sorry about this), companies don't care if you are loyal: they will still make you redundant if you are no longer needed.

This is not *unfair*, as such, because everyone is subject to the same indifference. But it can *feel* unfair at a fundamental level: there is a difference between things people know to be essentially important, such as loyalty and integrity, and what is actually held in high regard by the average company.

Stating that companies don't care is, of course, a bit daft. Companies *cannot* care. Companies aren't sentient: they're a gaggle of employees, a brand name and a legal entity logged somewhere in a database. The measure of a company is ultimately its P&L, and numbers aren't capable of caring. While an individual manager will certainly be aware of his or her employees' efforts, an employee who expects a company to display any reciprocal loyalty or memory, over the long term, is deluding themselves. In the words of Amy Poehler in her autobiography *Yes Please*: 'Depending on your career is like eating cake for breakfast and wondering why you start crying an hour later.'

However, even if there are attributes deep within you that companies are not structured to appreciate, there are plenty of measurable, tangible aspects of unfairness that organizations can act upon. For example, they can recruit fairly, and help people find the confidence to act like themselves rather than automatons. But how?

Rethinking recruitment

'We've welcomed poets, skaters, sculptors, jewellery designers, shelf stackers, artists and DJs through our doors,' said Andre Laurentino, speaking in 2020. Laurentino is not the director of an incredibly stylish artists' cooperative in East Berlin, but the CCO of creative experience agency Ogilvy UK, and he was referring to the company's groundbreaking internship scheme, known informally as 'The Pipe'.

Started in 2016 by group creative directors Johnny Watters and Angus George after they found that potential recruits tended to be 'generally white, middle class, university-educated males', The Pipe is a two-year apprenticeship blending work and study. It is open to all. It has no upper age limit and does not demand a degree, or even any relevant experience. 'University isn't for everyone,' Watters and George told website Creative Lives in Progress in 2019. 'Some of the most creative people in the world don't have an academic bone in their bodies. … Others simply can't afford it, and our industry misses out on all that talent.'

The application process is blind, as far as is possible: applicants initially submit a creative project with no other information about themselves. It doesn't matter if you have had a break in your past career, it only matters what you can offer *now*. The programme has seen pretty much everything, from a bumble bee piñata to a sequinned swimming costume. This initial stage is followed by a request for the applicant to try to sell a given object on Instagram – a used car, say, or a chair – and this stage is judged by a vote from everyone at Ogilvy. Only then do fifty candidates go in for speed interviews, where they meet with a wide range of staff members. Undeterred by the Covid-19 pandemic, the 2021 intake was determined by a remote assessment day instead.

Watters and George say of The Pipe: 'It's not about diversity for diversity's sake. All we care about is how they think. It's about diversity of thought.'

The great thing about such initiatives is that hiring based on aptitude, not professional background, benefits everyone in a business, not just the new recruits. It leads to a much less uniform intake of people, which leads in turn to a range of outlooks and working styles. This strikes me as an excellent way to reduce the risk of values-driven burnout. If there's no tedious norm one needs to conform to, a mask becomes pretty pointless.

I'm reminded again of my long-ago university summer job in the Chicago suburbs, where we each learned how to sell door-to-door by shadowing someone more experienced. My team leader, Jon Trigell, took me out on the road the day before we started work for real and showed me how to sell. It involved being very assertive and direct. This was a one-off deal. The person at the door, charmed by Jon's English accent and megawatt smile, would be crazy not to buy now.* If nothing else, I was a good student: I observed diligently. It's pretty likely that I made notes.

The next day I was on my own. I copied Jon's sales pitch word for word, knocked on thirty doors, and ... nothing. I was the only person in the whole division to fail to sell a single thing on their first day. And the next day was the same, too. And the one after that. I was starting to get pretty nervous by this point, because if I got fired, I would be alone on the wrong continent with a plane ticket home dated three months later.

On day four the division manager intervened. He put me under the wing of Sharon, a team leader with exactly the same amount of experience as Jon. As before, I was taken out on the road for a full day, while I observed Sharon selling. I quickly realized her approach was entirely different. Sharon tried to build a rapport with whoever answered the door. She mentioned having just chatted to their neighbours. She used humour to gently evade difficult questions. People would laugh and relax, and often they'd buy. She was being herself. They bought from Jon too – he was also being himself. But the two were very different.

The next day I was on my own again, but this time I took an approach that was much more like Sharon's. I chatted. I wasn't overly 'salesy'. I was surprised when I sold everything I had and more, taking orders for extra prints. By the end of the third week I was the top sales performer in the division. The sole difference was the opportunity to learn from someone whose approach suited my own.

People learn directly from their leaders. Sometimes you need to see a range of styles in order to realize there is more than one way of doing things; that you can probably accomplish a task

---

* Tellingly, Jon is now an award-winning author.

in a style that comes naturally to you rather than by imitating a certain norm.

Ideally, there would need to be no anxiety-inducing sense of difference between anyone's true self and their work self, and everyone could get on with their work as they see fit. It brings to mind the words of that foremost cultural authority Mrs Bird, speaking about London in the film *Paddington*: 'Everyone is different, and that means anyone can fit in.'

The advertising industry is fuelled by ideas, rather than a specific type of prior experience, so arguably it is an exception. But there are changes that can be made in more traditional recruitment processes. Returner schemes, for example, can be set up to target those who have had a break from a given industry. 'Every large company should offer one,' says returnee Tracy Jordan. 'They particularly help if someone has been out of an industry for longer than two to three years.'

Another possibility is to reduce the tick-box approach within the candidate application portal, if you have one. I've given up more than once out of sheer impatience with the labyrinthine hurdles of big company recruitment portals (no, I can't remember my user ID from eight years ago), and I'm someone who jumped obediently through most of the classic educational hoops. What if you can't tick all the boxes, and you're rejected without even having a conversation? Recruitment expert Nikolai Balzer agrees: 'With portals, you can't advocate verbally for a client who has any kind of non-standard employment history.' Portals therefore risk excluding good candidates at the first hurdle.

If your portal is not going anywhere in a hurry, though, request that a comments field is added so that recruiters can advocate for a candidate. Also try to develop good relationships with external recruiters: they know a good candidate when they see one, and they'll have talked with them in some depth before letting them near you.

The psychology of being a recruiting manager is also worthy of attention. Are managers made to feel like a failure if a new recruit doesn't work out within their trial period? Recruitment decisions are often as much about reducing personal risk as finding the right candidate. Recruiting managers who fear being judged are unlikely to stray far from the mould: do they want to be the person who hired the outlier?

Rory Sutherland, vice chairman of the ever-innovative Ogilvy, proposes recruiting batches of candidates at once. As he observes in his book *Alchemy: The Surprising Power of Ideas that Don't Make Sense*:

> If you hire one person and they go rogue, you have visibly failed. So, individuals who are hiring individuals may be unnecessarily risk averse.

Hiring a batch of people at once increases the chance that managers will take a chance on someone who doesn't fit the standard mould. Remarkably, years after Rory joined the organization he would one day help lead, he learned that he himself had benefitted from this approach:

> I would never have been offered a job had they been recruiting one person at a time, but because they had four vacancies they decided 'to take a punt on the wierdo', or words to that effect.

Or, consider emulating Google and taking the approach of having a batch of interviewers. Hiring decisions are made in a group to minimize the temptation for a manager to hire someone just like themselves, or to compromise because they need to fill a role urgently. This also helps neutralize the risks of 'gut feel' about the right cultural fit. While usually well intentioned, that's how you end up with a ton of people who all fit one particular mould.

Meanwhile, Ogilvy's scheme The Pipe has borne fruit. Junior creatives Lily James and Naomi Nicholl describe the opportunities made available to them while interns as 'almost comically enormous'. They worked on renowned brands and were even named as two of *Campaign* magazine's 'Faces to Watch' – 'all without needing a CV, or any experience'.

Andre Laurentino says of Ogilvy's programme: 'Since our first intake, Pipe members have won pitches, a Cannes Lion, D&AD and *The One Show* pencils, and, this year, a creative team made it into *Campaign*'s Faces to Watch list.' He goes on to add: 'If ours is a people business, we must act accordingly. Outsiders, welcome in.'

How about the other major issue of fairness: that of pay? Which companies are doing the right thing even when no one is looking?

Pay with principles

On the morning I meet up with Esther Chambers, an HR business partner at technology company Arm, I'm tired from wrangling with the topic of workplace fairness. Some of the research, on pay discrepancies in particular, is dispiriting and infuriating. I know Esther from working with her at QAS years ago. She's now in HR, and I want to know how she feels about the thorny topics of pay, loyalty and fairness. I order a large tea in the busy Cambridge cafe where we're meeting and sit myself down at a scrubbed pine table.

One hour and several cups of tea later, my faith in workplaces, and in humanity in general, has been restored. More than that, I want to apply for a job at Arm.

The Arm success story is renowned. Once described in the press as 'the biggest UK company you've never heard of', Arm processors power more than 180 billion devices worldwide. But what strikes me most during my chat with Esther is how passionately she speaks, unprompted, about fairness.

'We work really, really hard on fairness at Arm,' she tells me. 'Fair remuneration from the outset is really important because otherwise it all just chips away at trust. We do lots of work on this.'

'How, exactly?' I ask.

'We calibrate. The reward team looks at the salary ranges per role per location and reviews them regularly – a minimum of annually – in line with a number of benchmarks. On top there is a zero-tolerance approach to unexplained difference in pay. This is managed through a global fair pay analysis to make sure we haven't missed anything.'

Later, on the train home from Cambridge, I read about other companies that are working hard on fair pay. Some, such as the UK government funding consultancy GrantTree, even allow staff to choose their own salary. It's not a total free-for-all: employees do so by gathering market information, and their proposal is reviewed by colleagues in a transparent discussion.

Or take software firm Salesforce, which rates consistently highly in lists of top employers for its workplace culture. In 2015, when Salesforce chief people officer Cindy Robbins told CEO Mark Benioff that women in their firm were still being paid less than men, he found it hard to believe. Robbins and her team instigated an annual audit, which subsequently also calibrated by race and ethnicity. To date, the company has invested $10.3 million to correct pay disparities across similar roles. As Robbins told Inc.com in 2019: 'There's no excuse for any company to say, "Well, I can't do this, because I don't have the data behind it." Every company houses the data.'

Accounting software firm Intuit promotes a similar approach. Twice a year they conduct a pay equity analysis with an external company, reviewing pay by job code. As of August 2020 none of those job codes had significant differences between employees on the basis of gender or ethnicity.

You could argue that companies have to do this if they compete for talent – in the competitive tech market in Cambridge or London, say. But it's also simply the right thing to do, and it helps maintain a relationship of trust with each employee.

Companies that still think they can't afford this kind of largesse should assess the overall cost of losing someone and hiring afresh rather than just paying their original employee a fair rate.

Before leaving the cafe I ask Esther, 'What about the loyalty penalty?'

She grins: 'Internal moves have to be done fairly, too. It stores up such problems otherwise. Recently we discovered the market had changed for one type of role and we shifted the entire salary range as a one-off adjustment.'

This is doing the right thing even when no one is looking. When people know there is mutual trust and respect between themselves and their company, they are engaged and motivated to do their best. Ultimately, a fearless, focused and fair workplace environment is what will help make Sunday night dread a thing of the past.

Fairness: ideas

Ideas for the top

♦ Confident that you're fair already? You also have to *demonstrate* that you're fair. Always explain the company thinking and rationale. Leadership advisor Christie Hunter Arscott, writing in the *Harvard Business Review*, puts it well:

> Whether injustices are real or perceived, they have the same effect. ... When it comes to retaining talent, it does not matter what leaders think about their organization's compensation policy – the only thing that matters is what employees think about it.

♦ Scrap unfair and short-sighted constraints on pay rises for internal moves.

♦ Does your job specification really need to say 'PhD preferred' or 'MBA preferred', or is this just status-signalling on the part of your organization?

♦ Spell out what you're looking for in your next intake of managers. Make the hoops visible, such as influencing skills and presentation ability.

♦ Benchmark your salaries regularly by role, both for any imbalances and against the market.

WHY YOU DREAD WORK

♦ Managers will always spot the obvious contenders for leadership but those most eager for advancement are not necessarily the best leaders. Don't only develop those that shout the loudest.

♦ Don't favour tokenistic recognition schemes unless you are confident that your underlying pay structures are already fair. Small acts of recognition are great, but make sure they are not a hollow gesture.

♦ Wouldn't you like access to an until-now-overlooked talent pool? Don't dismiss those who've had breaks in their career.

♦ Put effort into hiring good recruiters.

Ideas for you

♦ Remember that leadership should be a two-way street: leaders are *there to help you* if there's something you can't fix with the resources available.

♦ Set up an informal buddy system for new starters so that new people do not mistakenly think everyone else knows everything.

♦ If you are a manager and you feel someone in your team is paid unfairly, be persistent on their behalf. Ask for benchmarking to be conducted by grade. Try to find allies. As Cindy Robbins told *The Observer* in 2019:

> Try finding co-workers who feel the same. It's more comfortable in many ways when it's not just one person going up a hill. You're all going up the hill together.

♦ Exclude the question, 'What do you currently earn?' when interviewing people. Instead focus on fair salary for the role.

♦ Take responsibility: remember, ultimately no one else is responsible for your happiness or your career path. If you think you need to leave to get what you want, then work towards doing so.

♦ If you are wearing a professional mask, consider taking it off. Colleagues come and go: who do you remember? It's usually the guy who kept bees, or the woman who was building her own house. Don't be a walking, talking LinkedIn profile. Life is too short.

Conclusion

While researching this book, I am delighted to discover one of those lengthy German compound nouns: *Sonntagsleerung*, which roughly corresponds to the idea of Sunday night dread. It dates from 1919, when the Hungarian psychoanalyst Sandor Ferenczi defined a malaise known as 'Sunday neuroses'. However, I note that Ferenczi's theory was that his subjects got ill or depressed on Sundays because the day offered too much time and freedom. I think it's safe to say that too much time and freedom is not the greatest concern of the modern employee.

Rather, modern employees are buffeted by a range of things that might induce a sense of dread: from difficult colleagues to an indifference to fairness. These things often play out quietly, so they silently impact engagement and productivity while people wonder if it's just them. However, one thing is clear: if you've ever been left feeling battle-scarred after another working week, you are not alone.

Happily, however, the elements of working life that trigger dread can be dialled down or even eliminated. These are not immutable, inevitable features of working life. And the exciting thing is that change can come from a variety of directions.

Switched-on executive boards know that happiness drives productivity, and can see that focusing only on visible outputs – 'what' gets done – is too limited a perspective. They know that there are other angles from which to view a healthy organization:

- Safety is the antidote to fear. To increase the sense of safety, companies need to look at '*How*'. What behaviour is acceptable in the pursuit of a goal? How can they inspire trust and goodwill?

- To help with focus, companies need to look also at 'Why'. Is this decision the best for the long term? Do those affected feel involved and listened to?
- And for greater fairness, look at 'Who'. Who is on the journey, and on what terms? Does the company do the right thing even when no one is looking?

Meanwhile, and perhaps more excitingly, change also comes from within ourselves. Yes, you can leave your job and run a llama-trekking retreat in deepest Wales (just bear in mind that, apparently, they spit). Or, you can take a fresh look at the bugbears of working life, and craft a better way to manage them:

- To help combat fear, decide how to handle conflict, and invest in friendship and affiliation. Presume goodwill in your interactions: these tiny changes have power.
- You can rediscover focus amid the chaos. Rethink your relationship with your workload and insist on gaps in your schedule for headspace and creativity. Think about your own sense of purpose.
- If your workplace feels unfair, change what you can control. Where there is imbalance of information, lobby for fairness. If you wear a mask, consider dropping it, if only to make the path easier for those that will come after you.

Despite the focus on numbers, budgets and balance sheets, it is clear that we experience our workplaces most viscerally through emotion and relationships. Dread is often driven by how someone else might react to something, or by doubt about your value relative to others. Even data overload is, at its heart, about interaction with others: behind every unread email is the dread of letting someone down. As impassive legal entities typically set up for profit, organizations often awkwardly coexist with the people that work within them. It's hardly surprising things get tricky.

And yet it is precisely that awkward undercurrent of emotion, flowing through the working week, that can lift a company to become greater than the sum of its parts. Intangible though it may be, a sense of trust drives affiliation, respect and goodwill for colleagues. Purpose gets people out of bed in the morning. Meanwhile, a level playing field of fairness makes it easy to focus on the ball, not the bumps in the field.

Of course, the ideal of a better working week sometimes feels complex to achieve, because it demands daily microdecisions from everyone involved. However, this also makes your workplace environment something dynamic and fluid, with endless capacity for reinvention and hope.

Wherever you work, eliminating Sunday night dread is an important aim. After all, the sum of your working weeks is a working life. And surely life is too short to spend it being anything other than happy and productive.

Dr Amy Edmondson, always gifted at thought-provoking statements, tells me, 'Most of us are waiting for an invitation to make a difference.' Consider this your invitation. When you're next at work, look around you. What's going well? What's going wrong? What could you change, today? Maybe we can banish Sunday night dread, together, one step at a time.

I wish you the very best of luck in your journey.

Acknowledgements

I owe lots of people a big thank you for their help with this book, most of all Sam, Diane and Richard at London Publishing Partnership. Thank you for your vision, patience and diligent editing-out of too many hyphens!

Thanks are also due to many others, including Jock Busuttil for reading an early draft, Simon Worth, David Birch, Claire Lowson, Esther Chambers and Tegwen at Arm, Dr Amy Edmondson, Sue Kay, Ellen Morgan for good company in glamorous locations, Rory Sutherland, Darren Irwin, Lisa Gill, Giles Turnbull, Dr Judith Mohring, Jen Edwards, Clive Smith, Nele van Hooste, Martina King, Charlotte Webb, Nick Jenkins, Martin Roll, Mathias Meyer, David Cote, James Anderson, Tom Caddick, Parul Sharma, Nikolai Balzer, Tracy Jordan, Katherine Gaylard, Olann Kerrison, Spiros Theodossiou and the former QAS Product Team for their skill at working out who married whom. Thanks are also due to Margaret McDonagh and Lorna Fitzsimons for their unswerving faith in a distinctly average alumnus of their Pipeline programme, and to all my amazing colleagues in past companies. To anyone who ever had to listen to me standing on a chair during a PI Planning session, my sincere apologies – I probably needed tea.

Most of all I owe a big debt of gratitude to my husband, Andy, for patiently getting two recalcitrant children to brush their teeth while I frowned at my laptop; and to my lovely children Lily and Anna, without whose homeschooling this book would have been finished a lot quicker.

References

All URLs correct as of 13 May 2021.

Introduction

Page 3 – In one 2019 survey, no less than 81%... TheSleepJudge Editorial Team. 2020. Sunday scaries. Online article, 4 November, TheSleepJudge.com (https://www.thesleepjudge.com/sunday-scaries/).

Page 4 – climate is more localized and ephemeral... Alvarez, A. 2020. Organizational culture vs. organizational climate. Online article, August, Caliper (https://calipercorp.com/blog/organizational-culture-vs-climate/).

Page 5 – a 'shadow side'... Tate, W. 2005. Working with the shadow side of organisations. Developing HR strategy. *Croner,* May. (Precis available at https://www.systemicleadershipinstitute.org/working-with-the-shadow-side-of-organisations-developing-hr-strategy-william-tate-croner-may-2005/.)

Page 5 – a 'shadow side'... Egan, G. 1994. *Working the Shadow Side: A Guide to Positive Behind-the-Scenes Management.* Jossey-Bass Management.

Chapter 1 – Other people

Page 11 – Michelle has said of her experience... Gordon, A. Undated. On the couch with Michelle Wolf. *Impose Magazine* (https://imposemagazine.com/bytes/humor/michelle-wolf-interview).

Page 12 – 96% of US employees... Porath, C. L., and Pearson, C. M. 2010. The cost of bad behavior. *Organizational Dynamics* **39**(1), 64–71 (https://doi.org/10.1016/j.orgdyn.2009.10.006).

Page 13 – 25% of managers who admitted to having... Porath, C. L., and Pearson, C. M. 2013. The price of incivility. *Harvard Business Review*, January–February (https://hbr. org/2013/01/the-price-of-incivility).

Page 16 – 3.9% of corporate professionals have psychopathic tendencies... Babiak, P., Neumann, G. S., and Hare, R. D. 2010. Corporate psychopathy, talking the walk. *Behavioral Science and the Law* **28**(2), 174–193.

Page 16 – compared to less than 1% in the general population... Coid, J., Yang, M., Ullrich, S., Roberts, A., and Hare, R. D. 2009. Prevalence and correlates of psychopathic traits in the household population of Great Britain. *International Journal of Law Psychiatry* **32**(2), 65–73 (https://doi.org/10.1016/j.ijlp.2009.01.002).

Page 16 – 'They don't usually end up in jail or psychiatric hospital...' Kets de Vries, M. F. R. 2012. The psychopath in the C suite: redefining the SOB. *SSRN Electronic Journal* (https://dx.doi. org/10.2139/ssrn.2179794).

Page 16 – It is even rumoured that some finance firms purposefully recruit social psychopaths... As told to the author. A similar statement was also quoted in Basham, B. 2011. Beware corporate psychopaths – they are still occupying positions of power. *The Independent,* 29 December (https://www.independent. co.uk/news/business/comment/brian-basham-beware-corporate-psychopaths-they-are-still-occupying-positions-power-6282502. html).

Page 17 – most employees concealed their feelings... Porath and Pearson (2010). The cost of bad behavior.

Page 17 – Sue Kay has studied bad behaviour at board level... Kay, S. 2014. 'Willful blindness' – narcissists at work. Executive Master's Thesis, INSEAD, Consulting and Coaching for Change (https://flora.insead.edu/fichiersti_wp/ InseadEMCCCtheseswave13/80371.pdf).

Page 17 – In his 2013 report commissioned by Barclays Bank...
Salz, A. 2013. Salz review: an independent review of Barclays'
business practices. Report (https://online.wsj.com/public/
resources/documents/SalzReview04032013.pdf).

Page 18 – Susan Fowler, formerly an engineer at Uber...
Fowler, S. 2017. Reflecting on one very strange year at Uber. Blog
post, 19 February (https://www.susanjfowler.com/blog/2017/2/19/
reflecting-on-one-very-strange-year-at-uber).

**Page 22 – One potential dividing line is introversion and
extroversion...** Graziano, W. G., Feldesman, A. B., and
Rahe, D. F. 1985. Extraversion, social cognition, and the
salience of aversiveness in social encounters. *Journal of
Personality and Social Psychology* **49**(4), 971–980 (https://doi.
org/10.1037/0022-3514.49.4.971).

**Page 22 – Lead researcher Markus Baer said of the
study...** Segran, E. 2014. Does workplace competition kill
women's creativity? *The Future of Work*, Fast Company
website, 15 August (https://www.fastcompany.com/3034477/
does-workplace-competition-kill-womens-creativity).

**Page 22 – In a study conducted by the Olin Business
School...** Baer, M., Vadera, A. K., Leenders, R. T. A. J., and
Oldham, G. R. 2014. Intergroup competition as a double-edged
sword: how sex composition regulates the effects of competition
on group creativity. *Organization Science* **25**(3), 892–908 (https://
doi.org/10.1287/orsc.2013.0878).

**Page 22 – One theory, discussed by Ashley Merryman and Po
Bronson...** Bronson, P., and Merryman. A. 2013. *Top Dog: The
Science of Winning and Losing*. Ebury Press, London.

Page 22 – An appetite, or otherwise, for competition... Guiso, L.,
and Rustichini, A. 2011. What drives women out of
entrepreneurship: the joint role of testosterone and culture.
Working Paper, European University Institute and EIEF, ECO
2011/2012. (Cited by Bronson and Merryman (2013).)

Page 23 – Companies like Amazon have dropped it...
González, A., and Day, M. 2016. Amazon to drop dreaded

stack-ranking performance reviews. *Seattle Times*, 14 November (https://www.seattletimes.com/business/amazon/amazon-says-it-will-change-performance-reviews-focus-on-staffers-strengths).

Page 23 – Companies like Microsoft have dropped it... Ovide, S., and Feintzeig, R. 2013. Microsoft abandons 'stack ranking' of employees. *Wall Street Journal*, 12 November (https://www.wsj.com/articles/SB10001424052702303460004579 193951987616572).

Page 23 – The Institute of Corporate Productivity reports that just 14% of companies... Jue, N. 2012. Four major flaws of force ranking. Online article, i4cp (https://www.i4cp.com/print/productivity-blog/2012/07/16/four-major-flaws-of-force-ranking).

Page 23 – 'Up or out' has also fallen out of favour... Cohan, P. 2012. Why stack ranking worked better at GE than Microsoft. *Forbes*, 13 July (https://www.forbes.com/sites/petercohan/2012/07/13/why-stack-ranking-worked-better-at-ge-than-microsoft/?sh=1189382f3236).

Page 23 – Take the work of Abraham Maslow... Maslow, A. H. 1943. *A Theory of Human Motivation*, eBook edition. Simon & Schuster (https://www.simonandschuster.co.uk/books/A-Theory-of-Human-Motivation/A-H-Maslow/9781627933964).

Page 23 – someone writing a business magazine article in the 1960s happened to draw it that way... Bridgman, T., Cummings, S., and Ballard, J. 2019. Who built Maslow's pyramid? A history of the creation of management studies' most famous symbol and its implications for management education. *Academy of Management Learning & Education* **18**, 81–98 (https://doi.org/10.5465/amle.2017.0351).

Chapter 2 – The price of fear

Page 25 – I had heard of 'fight or flight'... Cannon, W. B. 1927. The James–Lange theory of emotions: a critical examination and an alternative theory. *American Journal of Psychology* **39**(1/4), 106–124 (https://doi.org/10.2307/1415404).

Page 27 – All cruelty springs from weakness... Bulwer-Lytton, E. 1864. *Caxtoniana: A Series of Essays on Life, Literature, and Manners.* Harper & Brothers.

Page 27 – 90% of bullies have themselves been bullied... Gutman, L., and Brown, J. F. 2008. The importance of social worlds: an investigation of peer relationships. Research Report 29, Centre for Research on the Wider Benefits of Learning, Institute of Education, University of London (https://discovery.ucl.ac.uk/id/eprint/1541615/1/WLEreport29.pdf).

Page 27 – The more high-stakes, high-reward an industry... Berdahl, J. L., Cooper, M., Glick, P., Livingston, R. W., and Williams, J. C. 2018. Work as a masculinity contest. *Journal of Social Issues* **74**(3), 422–448 (https://doi.org/10.1111/josi.12289).

Page 28 – Sociologist Christin L. Munsch describes the masculinity contest... Munsch, C., Weaver, J., Bosson, J., and O'Connor, L. 2018. Everybody but me: pluralistic ignorance and the masculinity contest. *Journal of Social Issues* **74**, 551–578 (https://doi.org/10.1111/josi.12282).

Page 28 – manhood as 'elusive and tenuous'... Vandello, J., Bosson, J., Cohen, D., Burnaford, R., and Weaver, J. 2009. Precarious manhood. *Journal of Personality and Social Psychology* **95**(6), 1325–1339 (https://doi.org/10.1037/a0012453).

Page 28 – 48% of people who experience incivility... Porath and Pearson (2010). The cost of bad behavior.

Page 29 – Merely being around uncivil colleagues... Porath, C. L., and Erez, A. 2009. Overlooked but not untouched: how rudeness reduces onlookers' performance on routine and creative tasks. *Organizational Behavior and Human Decision Processes* **109**(1), 29–44 (https://doi.org/10.1016/j.obhdp.2009.01.003).

Page 29 – It's actually 'fight, flight, freeze or fawn'... Donahue, J. J. 2020. Fight–flight–freeze system. In *Encyclopedia of Personality and Individual Differences*, edited by V. Zeigler-Hill and T. K. Shackelford. Springer (https://doi.org/10.1007/978-3-319-24612-3_751). Walker, P. 2013. *Complex PTSD: From Surviving to Thriving.* CreateSpace.

Page 30 – In a 2016 interview with the Chartered Management Institute... Chartered Management Institute. 2016. Nick Leeson: poor management culture allowed me to fail. Interview, 19 February (https://www.managers.org.uk/knowledge-and-insights/interview/nick-leeson-poor-management-culture-allowed-me-to-fail/).

Page 31 – The related 245-page report... US House Committee for Transportation and Infrastructure. 2020. The design, development and certification of the Boeing 737 MAX. Final Committee Report, September (https://transportation.house.gov/imo/media/doc/2020.09.15%20FINAL%20737%20MAX%20Report%20for%20Public%20Release.pdf).

Page 32 – Michelle Wolf, the comedian, once said... Gordon, A. Undated. On the couch with Michelle Wolf. *Impose Magazine* (https://imposemagazine.com/bytes/humor/michelle-wolf-interview).

Page 36 – Rory Sutherland, vice-chairman of advertising agency Ogilvy... Sutherland, R. 2019. *Alchemy: The Surprising Power of Ideas that Don't Make Sense*. WH Allen, London.

Page 38 – a 27% reduction in attrition, 40% fewer safety incidents... Herway, J. 2017. How to create a culture of psychological safety. *Workplace*, 7 December, Gallup Inc. (https://www.gallup.com/workplace/236198/create-culture-psychological-safety.aspx).

Page 39 – 'Enjoyment appears at the boundary between boredom and anxiety...' Csikszentmihalyi, M. 2002. *Flow: The Psychology of Happiness*, 1st edition. Rider, London.

Page 40 – 'it is far safer to be feared than loved...' Machiavelli, N. 2009. *The Prince*, translated by P. Constantine. Vintage Classics, London.

Chapter 3 – Telling fear where to go

Page 43 – Their lightbulb moment, described in a 2016 *New York Times* article... Duhigg, C. 2016. What Google learned from its quest to build the perfect team. *New York Times*, 28 February, 'The Work Issue' (https://www.nytimes.com/2016/02/28/magazine/what-google-learned-from-its-quest-to-build-the-perfect-team.html).

Page 43 – 'A shared belief held by members of a team that the team is safe for interpersonal risk taking...' Edmondson, A. 1999. Psychological safety and learning behavior in work teams. *Administrative Science Quarterly* 44(2), 350–383 (https://doi.org/10.2307/2666999).

Page 45 – In a conversation for podcast Leadermorphosis... Gill, L. 2020. Amy Edmondson on psychological safety and the future of work. Leadermorphosis podcast, episode 45, 10 March (https://leadermorphosis.co/ep-45-amy-edmondson-on-psychological-safety-and-the-future-of-work).

Page 46 – At Spotify, some squads of engineers have 'fail walls'... Mankins, M., and Garton, E. 2017. How Spotify balances employee autonomy and accountability. *Harvard Business Review*, 9 February, Managing Organizations (https://hbr.org/2017/02/how-spotify-balances-employee-autonomy-and-accountability).

Page 46 – Accounting software firm Intuit reputedly gives a regular Failure Award... Stewart, H. 2015. 8 companies that celebrate mistakes. Blog post, 8 June, Happy (https://www.happy.co.uk/blogs/8-companies-that-celebrate-mistakes/).

Page 48 – 'Real change occurs from the bottom up; it occurs person to person...' Hawken, P. 2005. *Natural Capitalism: The Next Industrial Revolution*, 10th anniversary edition. Routledge.

Page 49 – On one visit to Chinese manufacturer Haier... De Morree, P. 2018. Promoting psychological safety in a Chinese manufacturing plant. Online article, Corporate Rebels (https://corporate-rebels.com/psychological-safety/).

Page 49 – In 2016, while working for the British Government Digital Service, consultant Giles Turnbull... Turnbull, G. 2016. It's ok to say what's ok. Blog post, 25 May, Government Digital Service (https://gds.blog.gov.uk/2016/05/25/its-ok-to-say-whats-ok/).

Page 51 – Nele van Hooste says of the taco feedback system...
Van Hooste, N. 2019. How we built a feedback culture with tacos, burgers and sushi. Blog post, Board of Innovation (https://www.boardofinnovation.com/blog/how-we-built-a-feedback-culture-with-tacos-burgers-and-sushi/).

Page 53 – Authors Rob Cross and Andrew Parker studied more than sixty informal networks... Cross, R., and Parker, A. 2004. *The Hidden Power of Social Networks: Understanding How Work Really Gets Done in Organizations*. Harvard Business Review Press, Cambridge, MA.

Page 53 – An alternative assessment of the organization chart...
Krackhardt, D., and Hanson, J. 1993. Informal networks, the company behind the chart. *Harvard Business Review* (https://hbr.org/1993/07/informal-networks-the-company-behind-the-chart).

Page 54 – Too many Zoom happy hours will lead to rebellion...
Matous, P., Pollack, J., and Helm, J. 2021. Collecting experimental network data from interventions on critical links in workplace networks. *Social Networks* **66**(July), 72–90 (https://doi.org/10.1016/j.socnet.2021.02.004).

Page 54 – Annamarie Mann, writing on the Gallup website...
Mann, A. 2018. Why we need best friends at work. *Workplace*, 15 January, Gallup Inc. (https://www.gallup.com/workplace/236213/why-need-best-friends-work.aspx).

Page 56 – One Glassdoor/MIT study found that investing...
Chamberlain, A., and Munyikwa, Z. 2020. What's culture worth? Stock performance of Glassdoor's best places to work 2009 to 2019. Economic Research, Glassdoor (https://www.glassdoor.com/research/app/uploads/sites/2/2020/04/Stock-Returns-2020-Glassdoor-Final-Reduced.pdf).

Page 58 – David Morrison, then Australia's Chief of Army, once said... Morrison, D. 2013 Chief of Army Lieutenant General David Morrison message about unacceptable behaviour. YouTube video (https://www.youtube.com/watch?v=QaqpoeVgr8U).

Page 59 – Netflix CEO Reed Hastings and INSEAD professor Erin Meyer write... Hastings, R., and Meyer, E. 2020. *No Rules Rules: Netflix and the Culture of Reinvention*. Virgin Books, London.

Page 59 – Airbnb has a week-long onboarding process... Suarez, P. 2019. How Airbnb fosters belonging in the workplace. Blog post, 21 February, Five to Nine (https://fivetonine.co/blog/ airbnb-belonging-workplace).

Page 63 – In one research study led by Adam Grant and Francesca Gino, being thanked... Grant, A., and Gino, F. 2010. A little thanks goes a long way: explaining why gratitude expressions motivate prosocial behavior. *Journal of Personality and Social Psychology* **98**(6), 946–955 (https://doi.org/10.1037/a0017935).

Chapter 4 – Data overload

Page 68 – In his sweeping history of humankind... Harari, N. Y. 2015. *Sapiens: A Brief History of Humankind*. Vintage, New York.

Page 69 – people spend around 80% of their work time answering... Cross, R., Rebele, R., and Grant, A. 2016. Collaborative overload. *Harvard Business Review*, January– February, Leadership & Managing People (https://hbr.org/2016/01/ collaborative-overload).

Page 69 – Just 3–5% of staff members contributed 20–35% of added value... Cross, Rebele and Grant (2016). Collaborative overload.

Page 71 – 'De-energizers'... Cross and Parker (2004). *The Hidden Power of Social Networks*.

Page 72 – Professor Nathanael Fast of the University of Southern California has examined this phenomenon... Fast, N. J., Halevy, N., and Galinsky, A. 2012. The destructive nature of power without status. *Journal of Experimental Social Psychology* **48**, 391–394.

Page 73 – In one study, 80% of employees lost work time... Porath and Pearson (2013). The price of incivility.

Page 73 – those experiencing rude emails had more trouble sleeping...   Yuan, Z., Park, Y., and Sliter, M. T. 2020. Put you down versus tune you out: further understanding active and passive e-mail incivility. *Journal of Occupational Health Psychology* **25**(5), 330–344 (https://doi.org/10.1037/ocp0000215).

Page 73 – And incivility tends to spread...   Rosen, C. C., Koopman, J., Gabriel, A. S., and Johnson, R. E. 2016. Who strikes back? A daily investigation of when and why incivility begets incivility. *Journal of Applied Psychology* **101**(11), 1620–1634 (https://doi.org/10.1037/apl0000140).

Page 73 – Task switching can incur costs of as much as 40% of productivity...   American Psychological Association. 2006. Multitasking: switching costs. Online article, 20 March (https://www.apa.org/research/action/multitask).

Page 73 – White-collar employees spend an average of nearly twenty-three hours a week in meetings...   Perlow, L. A., Noonan-Hadley, C., and Eun, E. 2017. Stop the meeting madness. *Harvard Business Review*, July–August, Meetings (https://hbr.org/2017/07/stop-the-meeting-madness).

Page 73 – 30% of workers said their workload was unmanageable...   Chartered Institute of Personnel and Development. 2018. UK working lives, from the CIPD Job Quality Index. 2018 Survey Report, CIPD (https://www.cipd.co.uk/Images/UK-working-lives-2_tcm18-40225.pdf).

Page 75 – In 1320 Dante Alighieri wrote his masterpiece...   Dante Alighieri. 2006. *Inferno*, translated and edited by R. Kirkpatrick. Penguin Classics, London.

Page 78 – 50% of millennials and 40% of Gen Xers felt pressure...   Curry, A., Hadidimoud, S., Raven, P. G., Siourakan, G., and Stubbs, J. 2017. Redefining the C-Suite: business the millennial way. Report, Kantar Futures on behalf of American Express (https://www.americanexpress.com/content/dam/amex/uk/staticassets/pdf/AmexBusinesstheMillennialWay.pdf).

Page 78 – You no doubt know Parkinson's Law...   Parkinson, C. B. 1955. Essay originally published anonymously in *The Economist*.

The Economist, 'From the Archive' (https://www.economist.com/ news/1955/11/19/parkinsons-law).

Page 78 – UK and US employees spend an extra two hours a day at their computer... Osborne, H. 2021. Home workers putting in more hours since Covid, research shows. *The Guardian*, 4 February (https://www.theguardian.com/business/2021/feb/04/ home-workers-putting-in-more-hours-since-covid-research).

Page 79 – Mathias Meyer, former CEO and cofounder of Travis CI, has written... Meyer, M. 2014. From open (unlimited) to minimum vacation policy. Blog post, 10 December (https://www. paperplanes.de/2014/12/10/from-open-to-minimum-vacation-policy.html).

Page 80 – In January 2021 an EU resolution was passed... European Parliament. 2021. 'Right to disconnect' should be an EU-wide fundamental right, MEPs say. Press Release, 21 January (https://www.europarl.europa.eu/news/en/press-room/20210114IPR95618/right-to-disconnect-should-be-an-eu-wide-fundamental-right-meps-say).

Page 80 – In 2021, 78% of respondents in a major survey in France... CGT. 2020. Enquête UGICT–CGT (UGICT–CGT survey). Online article, 12 May (https://www.cgt.fr/actualites/france/ interprofessionnel/conditions-de-travail/enquete-ugict-cgt).

Chapter 5 – What we can learn from freestyle rap

Page 81 – Allen Braun told *The Scientist*... Mole, B. M. 2012. Freestyle fMRI: brain scans of rap artists taken during improvised performances provide a snapshot of creative flow. *The Scientist*, 21 November (https://www.the-scientist.com/news-opinion/ freestyle-fmri-40159).

Page 81 – Braun and his team were examining the rappers... Liu, S., Chow, H. M., Xu, Y., Erkkinen, M. G., Swett, K. E., Eagle, M. W., Rizik-Baer, D. A., and Braun, A. R. 2012. Neural correlates of lyrical improvisation: an fMRI study of freestyle rap. *Scientific Reports* **2**, article 834 (https://doi.org/10.1038/srep00834).

Page 82 – One multinational study by the cognitive scientist Scott Barry Kaufman... Smith, J. 2016. 72% of people get their best ideas in the shower – here's why. *Business Insider*, 14 January (https://www.businessinsider.com/why-people-get-their-best-ideas-in-the-shower-2016-1?r=US&IR=T).

Page 83 – 'No one pursuit can be successfully followed by a man who is busied with many things...' Seneca. 2004. *On the Shortness of Life*, translated by C. D. N. Costa. Penguin, London.

Page 86 – the alleged telegram exchange in 1862 between French novelist Victor Hugo and his publisher... LaFrance, A. 2016. A surprise twist in the mystery of the lost telegrams. *The Atlantic*, 5 February (https://www.theatlantic.com/technology/archive/2016/02/telegrams-stop-found-stop-kinda/460161/).

Page 86 – Sandberg recounts in her book *Lean In*... Sandberg, S. 2015. *Lean In: Women, Work, and the Will to Lead*. W. H. Allen.

Chapter 6 – All change

Page 91 – Leadership consultant Jack Zenger writes in *Forbes*... Zenger, J. 2014. Individual contributors are forgotten leaders – are you developing them well? *Forbes*, 27 February, Leadership Strategy (https://www.forbes.com/sites/jackzenger/2014/02/27/individual-contributors-are-forgotten-leaders-are-you-developing-them-well/#3acda0d37469).

Page 91 – 'Restructuring disrupts the entire organization...' Sakpal, M. 2020. Organizational restructuring myths. Online article, Gartner, IT Leadership (https://www.gartner.com/smarterwithgartner/organizational-restructuring-myths).

Page 91 – The UK alone saw £83.4 billion of M&A activity in 2019... Office of National Statistics. 2020. Mergers and acquisitions involving UK companies, annual overview: 2019. Commentary, 3 March, Office for National Statistics (https://www.ons.gov.uk/businessindustryandtrade/changestobusiness/mergersandacquisitions/articles/ukmergersandacquisitionsactivityincontext/2019).

Page 91 – 83% of mergers failed to deliver shareholder value...
KPMG. 1999. Unlocking shareholder value: the keys to success.
Mergers and Acquisitions: A Global Research Report
(http://pages.stern.nyu.edu/~adamodar/pdfiles/eqnotes/
KPMGM&A.pdf).

**Page 92 – The London Stock Exchange ... higher-than-expected
cost to integrate financial data company Refinitiv...** Stafford, P.
2021. LSE Group shares suffer biggest daily fall in more
than 20 years. *Financial Times*, March (https://www.ft.com/
content/3cd149f6-8136-42bf-9319-e861c11a89ef).

**Page 92 – David Chancellor, writing for the Chartered
Management Institute...** Chancellor, D. 2015. 4 companies
that failed spectacularly, and the lessons of their demise. Case
Study, 17 September, Chartered Management Institute (https://
www.managers.org.uk/knowledge-and-insights/case-study/
four-companies-that-failed-spectacularly-and-the-lessons-of-their-
premature-demise/).

**Page 97 – Former CEO David Cote describes joining industrial
conglomerate Honeywell...** Cote, D. 2020. *Winning Now, Winning
Later: How Companies Can Succeed in the Short Term While
Investing for the Long Term.* HarperCollins Leadership, London.

**Page 99 – Of failed change efforts, no less than 39% had 'employee
resistance to change' as a factor...** Keller, S., and Price, C. 2011.
*Beyond Performance: How Great Organizations Build Ultimate
Competitive Advantage.* Wiley.

Page 101 – When Boeing merged with McDonnell Douglas...
US House Committee for Transportation and Infrastructure. 2020.
The design, development and certification of the Boeing 737 MAX.
Final Committee Report, September (https://transportation.
house.gov/imo/media/doc/2020.09.15%20FINAL%20737%20MAX%20
Report%20for%20Public%20Release.pdf).

Page 102 – Boeing issued a statement... Boeing Communications.
2020. Boeing statement on the House T&I Committee Report on
737 MAX. News Release, 16 September, Boeing (https://boeing.
mediaroom.com/news-releases-statements?item=130735).

Chapter 7 – More than money

Page 103 – Milton Friedman...   Friedman, M. 1970. The social responsibility of business is to increase its profits. *New York Times*, 13 September (https://www.nytimes.com/1970/09/13/archives/a-friedman-doctrine-the-social-responsibility-of-business-is-to.html).

Page 103 – 'Every quarter we felt pressure to find additional, potentially destructive solutions...' Cote (2020). *Winning Now, Winning Later.*

Page 104 – In one FCLT Global survey, 88% of executives agreed... Barton, D., Bailey, J., and Zoffer, J. 2016. Rising to the challenge of short-termism. Report, FCLT Global (https://www.fcltglobal.org/wp-content/uploads/fclt-global-rising-to-the-challenge.pdf).

Page 104 – In 2019, the median tenure of a CEO was just five years...   PWC Global. 2019. CEO turnover at record high; successors following long serving CEOs struggling according to PwC's Strategy & Global Study. Press Release, PwC (https://www.pwc.com/gx/en/news-room/press-releases/2019/ceo-turnover-record-high.html).

Page 104 – One report by management consultancy McKinsey... Birshan, M., Meakin, T., and Strovink, K. 2017. What makes a CEO 'exceptional'? Article, McKinsey & Company (https://www.mckinsey.com/business-functions/strategy-and-corporate-finance/our-insights/what-makes-a-ceo-exceptional).

Page 105 – Publicly traded US businesses scored lower on measures of integrity...   Guiso, L., Sapienza, P., and Zingales, L. 2013. The value of corporate culture. Working Paper, September, MIT (http://economics.mit.edu/files/9721).

Page 105 – All the homes had running water...   Sky History. Undated. Lord Leverhulme. Biography, Sky History (https://www.history.co.uk/biographies/lord-leverhulme).

Page 106 – He took his management team to Port Sunlight... Gelles, D. 2019. He ran an empire of soap and mayonnaise. Now he wants to reinvent capitalism. *New York Times*, 29 August (https://

www.nytimes.com/2019/08/29/business/paul-polman-unilever-corner-office.html).

Page 106 – 'If you buy into this long-term value-creation model...' Gunther, M. 2013. Unilever's CEO has a green thumb. *FORTUNE*, 23 May, Leadership: Global 500 (https://fortune.com/2013/05/23/unilevers-ceo-has-a-green-thumb/).

Page 106 – The *Financial Times* journalist Michael Skapinker was in the audience... Skapinker, M. 2018. Unilever's Paul Polman was a standout CEO of the past decade. *Financial Times* (https://www.ft.com/content/e7040df4-fa19-11e8-8b7c-6fa24bd5409c).

Page 106 – Interviewed five years later... Boynton, A., and Barchan, M. 2015. Unilever's Paul Polman: CEOs can't be 'slaves' to shareholders. *Forbes*, 20 July, Leadership (https://www.forbes.com/sites/andyboynton/2015/07/20/unilevers-paul-polman-ceos-cant-be-slaves-to-shareholders/?sh=26765759561e).

Page 107 – Since 2007 the association Business Roundtable... Business Roundtable. 2019. Business Roundtable redefines the purpose of a corporation to promote 'an economy that serves all Americans'. Press Release, August, Business Roundtable (https://www.businessroundtable.org/business-roundtable-redefines-the-purpose-of-a-corporation-to-promote-an-economy-that-serves-all-americans).

Page 107 – In mid 2020 Joe Biden... Yahoo! Life. 2020. Biden unveils economic plan, calls for end to shareholder capitalism. Video, July (https://www.yahoo.com/lifestyle/biden-unveils-economic-plan-calls-153218779.html?guccounter=1).

Page 107 – 75% of millennials expect their workplaces... Curry, A., Hadidimoud, S., Raven, P. G., Siourakan, G., and Stubbs, J. 2017. Redefining the C-Suite: business the millennial way. Report, Kantar Futures on behalf of American Express (https://www.americanexpress.com/content/dam/amex/uk/staticassets/pdf/AmexBusinesstheMillennialWay.pdf).

Page 107 – The Business Roundtable pledge has its critics... Winston, A. 2019. Is the Business Roundtable statement just empty rhetoric? *Harvard Business Review*, 30 August,

Economics & Society (https://hbr.org/2019/08/
is-the-business-roundtable-statement-just-empty-rhetoric).

Page 107 – By the time of David Cote's departure...
Smith, S. S. 2020. This CEO turned a money-losing firm into a $100
billion powerhouse. *Investor's Business Daily*, 30 July (https://
www.investors.com/news/management/leaders-and-success/
dave-cote-honeywell-former-ceo-bio-success/).

Page 108 – Cote insisted on intellectual rigour... Cote (2020).
Winning Now, Winning Later.

Page 108 – Firms with a long-term view outperformed...
Barton, Bailey and Zoffer (2016). Rising to the challenge of
short-termism.

**Page 108 – The faith of long-term investors in Unilever
was rewarded...** Unilever Press Office. 2018. Unilever CEO
announcement: Paul Polman to retire; Alan Jope appointed
as successor. Press Release, November, Unilever (https://
www.unilever.com/news/press-releases/2018/unilever-ceo-
announcement.html).

Page 108 – By 2012, the denim factory... Robinson, M.
2012. Interview with David Hieatt of Hiut Denim.
The 189, 2 March (https://the189.com/feature/
interview-with-david-hieatt-owner-and-founder-of-hiut-denim/).

Page 109 – Hiut Jeans supplies worldwide... Sheffield, H.
2018. Meghan Markle wore a pair of jeans made by Hiut, a
tiny Welsh denim company. Here's what happened next. *The
Independent*, 15 May (https://www.independent.co.uk/news/
business/indyventure/meghan-markle-hiut-jeans-denim-makers-
hieatt-a8281311.html).

Page 109 – 'We are clear in our mind...' Robinson (2012). Interview
with David Hieatt of Hiut Denim.

Page 109 – London-based company Envirobuild Materials...
Terrelonge, Z. 2017. Philanthropic 30 2017: the
most caring companies in Britain (10–1). *Real
Business*, 21 March (https://realbusiness.co.uk/
philanthropic-30-2017-caring-companies-britain10-1/).

Page 111 – Scott Keller and Mary Meaney... Keller, S., and Meaney, M. 2017. *Leading Organizations: Ten Timeless Truths.* Bloomsbury Business, London.

Page 115 – It resembles what social philosopher Charles Handy describes as a 'task culture'... Open University. Undated. Management: perspective and practice. OpenLearn (https://www. open.edu/openlearn/money-business/leadership-management/ management-perspective-and-practice/content-section-3.5.2).

Page115 – Psychologist Ellen Langer's classic research study... Langer, E., Blank, A., and Chanowitz, B. 1978. The mindlessness of ostensibly thoughtful action: the role of 'placebic' information in interpersonal interaction. *Journal of Personality and Social Psychology* **36**(6), 635–642.

Page 116 – 'Without involvement, there is no commitment...' Covey, S. 1989. *The 7 Habits of Highly Effective People.* Simon and Schuster, New York.

Page 117 – In one *Harvard Business Review* article... Brockner, J. 2006. Why it's so hard to be fair. *Harvard Business Review,* March, Organizational Culture (https://hbr.org/2006/03/ why-its-so-hard-to-be-fair).

Page 119 – Even 3M has to guard this time against profit pressure... Kretkowski, P. 1998. The 15 percent solution. *WIRED,* 23 January, Business (https://www.wired.com/1998/01/ the-15-percent-solution/).

Page 119 – The Post-It Note, of which 3M produces 50 billion a year... Glass, N., and Hume, T. 2013. The 'hallelujah moment' behind the invention of the Post-It Note. *CNN Business,* 4 April (https://edition.cnn.com/2013/04/04/tech/post-it-note-history/ index.html).

Page 120 – One McKinsey study found that only 10% of the fifty most value-creating roles... Dewar, C., Hirt, M., and Keller, S. 2019. The mindsets and practices of excellent CEOs. Article, 25 October, McKinsey & Company (https://www.mckinsey.com/ business-functions/strategy-and-corporate-finance/our-insights/ the-mindsets-and-practices-of-excellent-ceos).

Page 122 – mergers were 26% more likely than average to be successful... KPMG. 1999. Unlocking shareholder value: the keys to success. Mergers and Acquisitions: A Global Research Report (http://pages.stern.nyu.edu/~adamodar/pdfiles/eqnotes/KPMGM&A.pdf).

Chapter 8 – The fairness failure

Page 129 – Back in 1963 J. Stacey Adams developed his equity theory... Moniz Jr, R. J. 2010. Equity theory. *Science Direct* (https://www.sciencedirect.com/topics/social-sciences/equity-theory).

Page 130 – Students and staff at the Harvard School of Public Health... Solnick, S., and Hemenway, D. 1998. Is more always better? *Journal of Economic Behavior & Organization* **37**, 373–383 (https://www.albany.edu/~gs149266/Solnick%20&%20Hemenway%20(1998)%20-%20Positional%20concerns.pdf).

Page 132 – Women are four times less likely... Babcock, L., and Laschever, S. 2021. *Women Don't Ask: Negotiation and the Gender Divide*. Princeton University Press, Princeton, NJ.

Page 132 – Since 2017 in New York and some other US states it has been illegal... New York State. 2020. Salary history ban – what you need to know. New York State government website (https://www.ny.gov/salary-history-ban/salary-history-ban-what-you-need-know).

Page 134 – While gender pay gap reporting is mandatory in Britain... PA Media. 2020. UK 'unique in its light-touch approach' to gender pay gap. *The Guardian*, 14 October (https://www.theguardian.com/world/2020/oct/14/uk-unique-in-its-light-touch-approach-to-gender-pay-gap).

Page 134 – shocking gender pay gaps... Office for National Statistics. 2020. Gender pay gap in the UK: 2020. Report, ONS (https://www.ons.gov.uk/employmentandlabourmarket/peopleinwork/earningsandworkinghours/bulletins/genderpaygapintheuk/2020).

Page 135 – The company is left with the hefty cost of replacing them... Oxford Economics. 2014. The cost of brain drain: understanding the financial impact of staff turnover. Report, Oxford Economics (https://www.oxfordeconomics.com/recent-releases/the-cost-of-brain-drain).

Page 136 – Employees who previously trusted their organisation... Bianchi, E. C., Brockner, J., van den Bos, K., Seifert, M., Moon, H., van Dijke, M., and De Cremer, D. 2015. Trust in decision-making authorities dictates the form of the interactive relationship between outcome fairness and procedural fairness. *Personality and Social Psychology Bulletin* 41(1), 19–34.

Page 137 – If employees know their salary is low relative to their peers... Wikipedia. 2021. Performance-related pay. Article, Wikipedia (https://en.wikipedia.org/wiki/Performance-related_pay).

Page 137 – increased risk of sick days... Leineweber, C., Bernhard-Oettel, C., Peristera, P., Eib, C., Nyberg, A., and Westerlund, H. 2017. Interactional justice at work is related to sickness absence: a study using repeated measures in the Swedish working population. *BMC Public Health* 17, article 912 (https://doi.org/10.1186/s12889-017-4899-y).

Page 137 – heart rate variability, an early risk factor for coronary heart disease, increased... Falk, A., Kosse, F., Menrath, I., Verde, P. E., and Siegrist, J. 2014. Unfair pay and health. SOEP Papers on Multidisciplinary Panel Data Research, no. 715.

Page 138 – Employees who experienced bias were 60% more likely... Hewlett, S. A., Rashid, R., and Sherbin, L. 2017. When employees think the boss is unfair, they're more likely to disengage and leave. *Harvard Business Review*, 1 August, Managing People (https://hbr.org/2017/08/when-employees-think-the-boss-is-unfair-theyre-more-likely-to-disengage-and-leave).

Page 138 – people almost always leave for companies with a better culture... Chamberlain, A. 2018. Why employees quit you. YouTube video, 1 October, Glassdoor (https://www.youtube.com/watch?v=2MY42xhUDoY&t=1048s).

Chapter 9 – Who gets in – and who moves up

Page 139 – sociologist Michael Young...   Young, M. 1973. *The Rise of the Meritocracy, 1870-2033: An Essay on Education and Equality*, new impression edition. Penguin.

Page 140 – an overrated, ineffective and expensive barrier to entry...   Goodhart, D. 2020. Why universities had to be challenged. *UnHerd*, 14 July (https://unherd.com/2020/07/why-universities-had-to-be-challenged/).

Page 142 – a mother's earnings fall sharply after the first child... Scott, L. 2020. How coronavirus is widening the UK gender pay gap. *The Guardian*, 7 July (https://www.theguardian.com/world/2020/jul/07/how-coronavirus-is-widening-the-uk-gender-pay-gap).

Page 144 – what matters is not the policy...   Williams, J. C. 1999. *Unbending Gender: Why Family and Work Conflict and What to Do About It*. Oxford University Press.

Page 148 – give yourself permission to 'waste' five percent of your day...   Frankel, L. P. 2014. *Nice Girls Don't Get The Corner Office: Unconscious Mistakes Women Make that Sabotage Their Careers*. Grand Central, New York.

Chapter 10 – Please wear a mask

Page 149 – 61% of respondents admitted to...   Smith, C., Yoshino, K., and Levit, A. 2013. Uncovering talent: a new model of Inclusion. Report, December, Deloitte (https://www2.deloitte.com/content/dam/Deloitte/us/Documents/about-deloitte/us-about-deloitte-uncovering-talent-a-new-model-of-inclusion.pdf).

Page 149 – the drive for authenticity as a Western phenomenon... Henrich, J. 2021. *The Weirdest People in the World: How the West Became Psychologically Peculiar and Particularly Prosperous*. Penguin.

Page 153 – should read *Quiet* by Susan Cain... Cain, S. 2013. *Quiet: The Power of Introverts in a World that Can't Stop Talking*. Penguin.

Page 153 – Google's Project Aristotle looked at extroversion... Google. Undated. Guide: understand team effectiveness. Online article, re:Work (https://rework.withgoogle.com/print/guides/5721312655835136/).

Page 154 – masculinity contest cultures (referenced in chapter 3) were prone to pluralistic ignorance... Munsch, C. L., Weaver, J. R., Bosson, J. K., and O'Connor, L. T. 2018. Everybody but me: pluralistic ignorance and the masculinity contest. *Journal of Social Issues* **74**(3), 551–578.

Page 156 – burnout was recognized as an occupational phenomenon... Danaher, M. 2019. The World Health Organization is focusing attention on workplace burnout, and so should employers. *Employment Law Matters*, 6 June (https://www.employmentlawmatters.net/2019/06/articles/ada/the-world-health-organization-is-focusing-attention-on-workplace-burnout-and-so-should-employers/).

Page 156 – Depending on the attribute being masked, between 60% and 73% of respondents... Smith, Yoshino and Levit (2013). Uncovering talent: a new model of Inclusion.

Page 156 – the respected Maslach Burnout Inventory... Maslach, C., and Jackson, S. E. 1981. The measurement of experienced burnout. *Journal of Organizational Behavior* **2**(2), 99–113 (https://doi.org/10.1002/job.4030020205).

Page 157 – McKinsey report that 75% of Americans... *Better Bosses*. McKinsey (https://www.mckinsey.com/business-functions/organization/our-insights/five-fifty-better-bosses).

Page 158 – 'Most leaders delegate complexity downward...' Kingston, S. 2020. Why purpose-driven leadership matters now more than ever: a Q&A with Paul Polman. Insights, 22 April, Russell Reynolds (https://www.russellreynolds.com/insights/thought-leadership/why-purpose-driven-leadership-matters-now-more-than-ever-a-qa-with-paul-polman).

Page 158 – Mel MacIntyre, a business coach, had a similar experience... Saner, E. 2021. A career change saved my life. *The Guardian*, 8 June (https://www.theguardian.com/lifeandstyle/2021/jun/08/a-career-change-saved-my-life-the-Page 30 – people-who-built-better-lives-after-burnout).

Page 158 – neurological damage... Michel, A. 2016. Burnout and the brain. *Psychological Science*, 29 January (https://www.psychologicalscience.org/observer/burnout-and-the-brain).

Page 158 – Those in the top 20% for burnout symptoms... Toker, S., Melamed, S., Berliner, S., Zeltser, D., and Shapira, I. 2012. Burnout and risk of coronary heart disease: a prospective study of 8838 employees. *Psychosomatic Medicine* **74**(8), 840–847 (https://doi.org/10.1097/psy.0b013e31826c3174).

Chapter 11 – Making fairness fundamental

Page 161 – Résumé virtues and Eulogy virtues... Brooks, D. 2016. *The Road To Character*, 1st edition. Penguin.

Page 162 – Depending on your career... Poehler, A. 2015. *Yes Please*, main market edition. Picador.

Page 162 – 'We've welcomed poets, skaters...' Pumpkin. 2020. Ogilvy unveils 'nominate that mate' recruitment campaign to launch 2021 apprenticeship scheme – The Pipe. *BDaily News*, 11 November (https://bdaily.co.uk/articles/2020/11/11/ogilvy-unveils-nominate-that-mate-recruitment-campaign-to-launch-2021-apprenticeship-scheme-the-pipe).

Page 162 – Started in 2016 by group creative directors Johnny Watters and Angus George... Watters, J., and George, A. 2019. Inside The Pipe, Ogilvy's unconventional creative internship programme. *Creative Lives in Progress*, 17 June (https://www.creativelivesinprogress.com/article/ogilvy-the-pipe).

Page 166 – Recruiting batches of candidates at once... Sutherland, R. 2019. *Alchemy: The Surprising Power of Ideas that Don't Make Sense*. WH Allen, London.

Page 166 – the approach of a batch of interviewers... Bryant, A. 2011. Google's quest to build a better boss. *New York Times*, 13 March (https://nytimes.com/2011/03/13/business/13hire. html?smid=pl-share).

Page 166 – Junior creatives Lily James and Naomi Nicholl... Pumpkin (2020). Ogilvy unveils 'nominate that mate' recruitment campaign to launch 2021 apprenticeship scheme – The Pipe.

Page 168 – GrantTree even allow staff to choose their own salary... Kellner, R. 2018. I set my own salary: it blows people's minds. Online article, 16 October, GrantTree (https://granttree. co.uk/i-set-my-own-salary-it-blows-peoples-minds/).

Page 168 – Cindy Robbins told CEO Mark Benioff... Fletcher, P. 2015. Salesforce and equal pay: the tech giant is putting its money where its mouth is. *The Guardian*, 23 November (https://www. theguardian.com/women-in-leadership/2015/nov/23/salesforce-and-equal-pay-the-tech-giant-is-putting-its-money-where-its-mouth-is).

Page 168 – $10.3 million... Prophet, T. 2019. Our path to equality: the Salesforce annual update. Blog post, November, Salesforce (https://www.salesforce.com/blog/equality-annual-update/).

Page 168 – 'There's no excuse for any company to say...' Downes, S. 2019. How to fix gender inequality at your company, from the HR exec who helped close Salesforce's pay gap. *Inc.*, 12 September, Company Culture (https://www.inc.com/sophie-downes/salesforce-cindy-robbins-gender-pay-gap-equity-parity-salary-compensation.html).

Page 168 – Accounting software firm Intuit promotes a similar approach... Intuit. Undated. Diversity, equity and inclusion at Intuit. Online article (https://www.intuit.com/ca/company/corporate-responsibility/diversity/).

Page 171 – Leadership advisor Christie Hunter Arscott... Hunter Arscott, C. 2016. Pay fairness isn't just about teaching employees to negotiate. *Harvard Business Review*, 4 May. Compensation (https://bg.hbr.org/2016/05/pay-fairness-isnt-just-about-teaching-employees-to-negotiate).

Conclusion

Page 175 – *Sonntagsleerung...* Ferenczi, S. 1969. *Further Contributions to the Theory and Technique of Psycho-Analysis*, 3rd edition. Institute of Psycho-analysis.

Index